THE MEANING AND
SIGNIFICANCE OF DREAMS

C.A. Meier

translated by
David N. Roscoe

SIGO PRESS
BOSTON

⬤ SIGO PRESS
25 New Chardon Street, # 8748
Boston, Massachusetts 02114

Publisher and General Editor: Sisa Sternback

Library of Congress Cataloging in Publication Data

Meier, C. A. (Carl Alfred), 1903-
   The meaning and significance of dreams.

   (The Psychology of C. G. Jung ; v. 2)
   Translation of: Die Bedeutung des Traumes.
   Bibliography: p.
   Includes index.
   1. Dreams.   2. Jung, C.G. (Carl Gustav), 1875-1961--
Contributions in interpretation of dreams.   I. Title.
II. Series: Meier, C.A. (Carl Alfred), 1903-
Lehrbuch der komplexen Psychologie C. G. Jung.
English ; v. 2.
BF173.J85M43513   1984 vol. 2   150.19'54 s   87-12825
[BF1078]   [154.6'3]
ISBN 0-938434-11-X
ISBN 0-938434-69-1 [pbk]

Set in English Times.
Printed in the United States of America on acid free paper.

Carolyn M. Bates PhD
4131 Spicewood Springs K-8
Austin, Texas 78759

THE MEANING AND
SIGNIFICANCE OF DREAMS

TABLE OF CONTENTS

LIST OF ILLUSTRATIONS

To my wife,
our children and their children

"Ego dormio sed cor meum vigilat"
Canticus IV.1.2

FOREWORD

*"Man muss tüchtig geboren sein, um ohne
Kränklichkeit auf sein Inneres
zurückzugehen."*[1] Gesundes Hineinblicken in
sich selbst, ohne sich zu untergraben;
nicht mit Wahn und Fabelei, sondern mit
reinem Schauen in die unerforschte Tiefe
sich wagen, ist eine seltene Gabe, aber
auch die Resultate solcher Forschung für
Welt und Wissenschaft ein seltenes Glück.
—Goethe, 1819

Throughout his life, Carl Gustav Jung was intensively involved
with his patients' dreams, and with utter conviction, so that one may
safely assume that he had fully adopted Freud's legendary phrase
that the dream is the *via regia* to the unconscious. Considering that
he has made a great deal of his practical experience accessible to
those around him, in his extensive publications, it comes as a surprise to observe that remarkably little space is devoted to the dream
in Jung's writings. There are in fact four very short works on the
subject of the dream.[2]

True, he did occasionally voice the opinion that it is not the dream
but the active imagination that is the real *via regia* to the unconscious. But it is not the aim of this volume to deal with that specifically Jungian technique, the problem of the dream being difficult
and complex enough in its own right.

It is nevertheless to be regretted that we have no extensive and
comprehensive treatment of the dream from Jung's own pen. Fortunately, however, in his seminars at the E.T.H. he constantly
turned to the dream, and I am in the happy position of having

ix

received from him his notes on the subject. This was after I had begun to succeed him at the E.T.H., first as his assistant and later working independently. Much of what I shall say in this volume is thus a reflection of authentic Jungian views. In saying this, I am not trying to cover myself for what I have written here, but rather expressing my gratitude for Jung's generosity.

The deeper reason why we have nothing more detailed on the subject from Jung is probably that there is hardly a more complex feature of the human psyche than the dream. Even today we do not have the overview to enable us to convey the contents of the vast material I have (a collection of some 50,000 dreams). The first valid attempt to use statistical evaluation to draw viable conclusions on the contents and subject matter of average dreams was made by Hall and Van der Castle.[3] Once we have the baseline for dreams that occurred under natural conditions, then we will be in a position to evaluate deviations quantitatively and qualitatively and assign to them their due value. But that will still take years. For a long time to come we will depend on much-acclaimed experience, on psychological intuition and on more or less plausible conjectures. For until we know how banal (i.e., common) a certain dream motif is, we cannot assess its significance or "valuelessness."

I would have to lay down my pen at this point, and practice patience, if the phenomenology of dreams were not so fascinating in itself that the scientific thirst for knowledge is constantly challenged by it, and the situation is still felt to be highly unsatisfactory. So it is not easy just to stick to the old school.

Part of the "old school" is undoubtedly Freud's monumental pioneer work *The Interpretation of Dreams*.[4] Without wishing to cast aspersions on the master's achievement, it must be said that in support of his new hypothesis he had to leave out a lot which would be an integral part of a complete description of this incredibly complex phenomenon. It is precisely because of the complicated nature of a factual situation that one is obliged to resort to simplification at first, and, as Freud's example has shown, there is no reason why this should not be fruitful. Jung nevertheless posed some of the questions that kept cropping up. But he left them open and thus did not feel in a position to develop a total view.

It was only just before Jung's death that modern experimental biology began to develop new approaches to sleep and dreams, the consequences of which cannot yet be foreseen. But in the future it will be impossible to omit them from any total view of the dream. Jung's prudent caution justifies itself *a posteriori* for this reason alone, and it is to be hoped that in the longer-term future, many a new aspect will emerge with regard to the understanding of dreams.

But we do believe that Jung put forward several significant suggestions[5] in response to the many questions about dreams which remain open, apart from Freud, and for this very reason it is necessary to make a hitherto unattempted effort to present an overview of his point of view.

CHAPTER I

BASIC FACTS ABOUT
THE METHODOLOGY

"We are such stuff
As dreams are made on; and our little life
Is rounded with a sleep."
—Shakespeare,
The Tempest, Act IV, Sc.i, 156–158

In the field of psychology it has become the custom to set the phenomenon to be investigated against a comparative and historical point of view. This procedure has several arguments in its favor.

First, because the psyche—and the unconscious in particular—is by definition the most unknown of all entities, we should try to avoid any preconceived opinions on the subject. It can be helpful, however, to find out how certain terms or concepts have developed over the centuries.

Second, the psyche is the real constant in human nature and has remained the same, *mutatis mutandis*, at all times and in all places. We can find nothing new in the most recent developments in the history of mankind. What is new in any individual case is just one step more in the naturally prescribed growing consciousness of the individual. Creative achievements are no exception but prove to be mere general or generally valid truths of temporary significance. Seen in this relativization, a "Dream Science"[6] is certainly possible, at least insofar as it represents a thorough collection of the knowledge of the material already available. But openmindedness

1 *to multiple hypotheses*

must prevail at all times, a quality unfortunately lacking in many Freudians. What can be overlooked in Freud, with his justifiable eagerness for discovery, does not apply to his successors, who, regrettably, cling to the old scheme of things despite many new findings.

Third, the consensus gentium may be supposed to be a mirror of the everywhere-identical human soul, so that what it has to say must somehow correspond to the psychic facts and thus have the right to be taken seriously.

Thus we have grounds for looking at a wide spectrum of people and ages and seriously considering what they have experienced and thought about dreams. Of course, a comprehensive assessment of the dream theories of all cultures would be desirable, but would be too much for any one individual. A thorough knowledge of the anthropology, culture and religion of these peoples would be needed. Hence in the comparative-historical section of this work we content ourselves with just a few examples of peoples who are already well known to us, and whose sources can be translated into our contemporary psychological language relatively easily.

It is true that we now have dream research based on science, in fact on natural science. But its authors, jealously clinging to their scientific approach, refuse to go into the *meaning* of dreams. We hear a lot from them about the neurophysiological conditions, about the brain structures involved, and similar biological factors connected with dreams. We also learn the surprising fact that everybody regularly dreams four to six times a night, at rhythmic intervals, whether they remember it or not. We also hear that experimental interruption of dreaming has unpleasant effects and produces a need to make up for the loss of dreams. This last fact, which is well proven, clearly shows that the dream at least represents a biological necessity.

All this is very important but gets us no nearer to answering the question of Nicodemus about what dreams actually *mean*. The natural scientist is not interested in the meaning of a phenomenon. Yet ancient respect for the dream among all peoples and at all times is based on their shared conviction that it is imbued with meaning.

Scientific psychology deals almost exclusively with the phenomenon of consciousness, whereas the dream is a select product of the unconscious psyche. As a spontaneous product of nature, the dream obeys laws different from those governing a product of consciousness. But we can discover the laws, i.e., constant relationships, in the dream, when we see it as a product of nature.

In Volume I of this textbook, we dealt with processes in which the unconscious psyche plays a crucial role. This is much the case with the dream, in that it only comes about *"in unbewussten Momente"* (Goethe)—i.e., in sleep. The dream can, in fact, be understood as the almost undisturbed activity of the unconscious, a view supported by the experimental findings of Aserinsky,[7] Kleitman and Dement,[8] which show that everybody—perhaps even all higher vertebrate animals—dreams regularly while sleeping, even when they do not remember dreaming.

Despite the possibilities for experimental objectivization of the dream cited by these writers, we are still a long way from understanding why certain dreams are remembered and others not. It must be assumed that for recollection there is a residual consciousness. But that is just sufficient for the understanding of memorability as such. Objective significance can hardly be attributed to it, and this is equally true for the fixtures of the dream laboratory (cf. Chapter II, Sec. 4). Even if the electric signals of the brain could be deciphered during dreaming, causing the dream to appear simultaneously on a screen, the main difficulty would remain: the archimedal point outside the unconscious psychic system of the dreamer would still be missing.

In this respect we find ourselves in a situation similar to the problem of the cut between the observer and the system observed, the famous problem in physics of the subject/object relation. For a psychology of the unconscious processes is nothing more than a heroic attempt to place the cut between subject and object as far as possible into the object. In psychology the subject (the psyche of the observer) is purely psychical and internal, whereas in the laboratory situation referred to, the object is partly physical-objective and external. Between the two there is a kind of indeterminacy relation (Heisenberg), for the more precisely the one is defined, the more imprecise become the dimensions of the other. This is true even to the extent that any over-intimate interference of the subject in the object disturbs the latter in such an uncontrollable fashion that it is totally obliterated.

People who are particularly keen to grasp their dreams actually chase them away with this attitude. And with Freud, too, suppression or censorship (both offspring of consciousness) is responsible for people forgetting dreams. We may even assume that as neurophysiological investigations become more and more refined, we will actually upset or even destroy the dream phenomenon, replace it with more and more rudimentary affects, and become less and less able to comment on the phenomenon to be examined. These considerations occasioned Niels Bohr,[9] as early as 1933, to extend his idea of complementarity in the relationship between physics and psychology. Here are some of his most important comments on this subject: .

> The continuity of light production in time and space, on the one hand, and the atomic nature of the light effects on the other must thus be seen as complementary sides of one and the same thing, in that each one brings out important features of the phenomena of light. These phenomena, even if they are irreconcilable from the point of view of mechanics, can never be placed in direct opposition, since a thorough analysis of one or other characteristic on the basis of mechanical concepts calls for various ways of attempting to categorize them that are mutually exclusive. . .
>
> . . . Thus there exists a complementary relationship between that unequivocal use of the term of stationary state and a mechanical analysis of the movements of the particles within the atom, and this relationship corresponds exactly to the behaviour described between light quanta and the electro-magnetic theory of radiation. . .
>
> . . . Just as the term relativity indicates the fundamental dependence of the physical phenomena on the reference system used to place it in time and space, so the term complementarity serves as a symbol for the limitation that emerges in atomic physics, namely a limitation of our usual conception of an existence of the phenomena that is independent of the means of observation. . .
>
> . . . In our treatment of the question of the application of mechanical terms with living organisms, we looked at them just as other material objects. However, I hardly need emphasize that this attitude, which is typical of physiological investigation, in no way ignores the psychological processes linked to life. It is much rather the case that the acknowledgment of the limitation of the mechanical concepts in atomic physics seems suited to reconciling the apparently contradictory points of view that characterize physiology and psychology. For the necessity in atomic mechanics of taking into consideration the reciprocal effect between measuring instruments and the object under examination recalls the innate difficulties which we find in psychological analysis, which stem from the fact that the content of the conscious changes as soon as an attempt is made to direct attention to one of its elements.

In 1950 W. Pauli[10] expressed himself as follows on the subject:

> On the one hand modern psychology can show a largely objective reality of the unconscious psyche; on the other hand, any consciousness raising, i.e., observation, represents a basically uncontrollable

intrusion into the unconscious content, whereby the objective nature of the reality of the unconscious places limits, and at the same time loses in objectivity.

From this it can be deduced that in this subject/object relation we would, through undaunted cut after cut into the object, ultimately come up against the psyche in physics, and physics in psychology. Thus in a somewhat complicated fashion, we have expressed the long-known fact that the psychic can only be observed and expressed with psychic means. This reminds us of a remark made by Schelling[11]:

> This eternal unconscious, like the eternal sun in the realm of the spirits, hides itself through its own serene light and, although it never becomes an object, stamps its identity on all free actions. And it is at once the same for all forms of intelligence, the invisible roots, of which all intelligences are merely the powers and the eternal conveyer of the self-defining subjective within us, and the objective or the onlooker, at once the basis of legality in freedom and freedom in legality.

The psychologist of today, too, with his scientific approach, need not yet say "ignorabimus." A number of methods of dream research can take us at least a few steps further. We shall be looking at them in the following chapters.

CHAPTER II

METHODS OF
DREAM RESEARCH

1. Rational Methods

Insofar as we are aware of the basically unavoidable difficulties mentioned in Chapter I, we must, for the time being, resort to indirect methods. What spring to mind here are comparative points of view. For example, we can attempt to grasp the unconscious products of the dream with the resources of the conscious, set up in relation to the conscious, i.e., take the conscious into consideration as a contributory factor. This can take place in the following two ways, for example:

(a) Comparison between the imaginative process in the conscious in general, and the imaginative process in the dream. Such comparisons have been made on an intensive level by Emil Kraepelin in his work *Die Sprachstörungen im Traum*.[12] On an extensive level, there is the attempt made by K. Leonhard, entitled *Die Gesetze des normalen Träumens*.[13] A similar attempt was made by Robert Bossard in *Psychologie des Traumbewusstseins*.[14] Clearly such a method of observation could only carry weight if it is carried out on the basis of a sufficient number of dreams to allow for a statistical evaluation. It should then theoretically be possible to draw comparisons, in the way that Freud did, purely intuitively. Unfortunately, in his case one aspect of the comparison is always sexuality, although here it must be assumed that with this form of *petitio principii*, the theory was influenced by his own psychology. So one should be wary of jumping to conclusions with these comparisons.

6

(b) Comparison of the dream concept with the individual consciousness situation and the dreamer's actual situation. The bases for this method of observation are best sought in extreme cases, which is why such investigations were usually carried out by doctors who made use of the material they had in the form of their patients. When, for example, a patient has pronounced inferiority feelings, his dream material can be investigated to see how this situation is reflected. Moreover, this method can be used to investigate at which points in the dream series certain motifs appear in frequencies. These frequencies can be examined and it can be ascertained with which frequencies of the dreamer's consciousness concepts or his external reality situation they coincide.

Jung used this method to look at his dream material, and gave specific names to the frequencies of certain dream figures and motifs. Examples are "shadow," "anima," "mandala," and so on. In this respect one should make a comparison with *Dream Symbols of the Individuation Process*,[15] where Jung makes an initial statistical principle of this nature, and also with *Psychology and Alchemy*.[16]

Of course, methods 1(a) and 1(b) call for a large number of dreams if reasonably reliable correlations are to emerge. The process is a rational one in that it assumes what is being dealt with is the relationship between two well-known dimensions, or at least between a well-known one and one that is comparable.

2. Amplification Method

The treatment of the dream by use of amplification is a method inaugurated by Jung. It is not so suitable for just any dream, but rather for those where other methods have not proved satisfactory. Moreover, it is confined to individual dream elements, to which the dreamer can recall few or no personal experiences, and which yet play a vital role in the dream text. Amplification is classically applied to elements which stand out because of their alien character. The meaning in such pictures, however, is not recognized, because it is often a matter of hints, terse expressions, or fragmentary statements.

When philologists come across a newly discovered tattered ancient text, they usually embark on its reconstruction by making conjectures based on analogous passages where the corresponding parts are better preserved. This is essentially the procedure in the amplification method. We deal with the corresponding incomprehensible dream element as if it were a gap in an otherwise reasonably well-preserved text, taking pains, of course, to remain in the milieu in which the corresponding dream motif is embedded. In contrast to the two methods previously mentioned, with amplification we remain with the individual case and try to extend it (lat: *amplificare*, from *amplus* + *facio* = extend, stretch, increase, raise, shed clearer light on). Amplification as a method thus certainly remains with the same object, i.e., the psychic content of the dream. It seeks not so much to connect the content of the dream with the consciousness of the dreamer, as to remain within the unconscious, so that the subject/object relation presents no major problem.

Once this amplification work has been done, it can happen that the *meaning* of the dream setting emerges as a new element, and thus its connection with the consciousness of the dreamer will become clear. It emerges then of its own accord, to a certain extent, as a consequence of the amplification, and this relationship can actually appear as a new kind of experience, with a consciousness-transforming effect, which, *ea ipsa*, is convincing. Unfortunately this method is not suited to an abstract demonstration, as the immediately convincing effect is an intensely subjective process. This is why its focal point is in therapy, which is not our topic here. However, as most psychological attitudes in which the phenomena of the unconscious play an important role show their greatest effects in the field of psychopathology, it is worthwhile illustrating the method here with one such example. To do this we need a brief previous history of the case. I include only the data necessary to examine one special dream.

The patient, who was 57 years old at the time, was a successful American lawyer, who held several important positions. He was happily married and had two children. For several years he had been suffering from severe mental depression and had spent time in several American sanatoriums, but to no avail. At that time there were no psychopharmacologic drugs and the only known treatment for depression was insulin shock; however, this method was not used.

He was paralyzed both psychically and physically and could hardly be persuaded to talk. It was in this condition that he appeared in my consulting room, almost dragged along by his wife. He could barely answer the few questions I asked him, and so all I did was to give him a short talk on the possible psychological factors in such a condition and how these could manifest themselves in dreams. According to what the patient himself said, he had not yet had any dreams. At the close of the session I asked him to please pay attention to his dreams.

He appeared for the second time two days later, bearing a sheet of paper on which he had dictated to his wife the first of his dreams. This is how it went:

> I was fishing for trout, not in an ordinary river or lake but in a reservoir, which was divided up into various compartments. I was using ordinary fishing tackle (flies, etc.). I was having no luck. As I was growing angry and impatient, I picked up a trident that was lying there and immediately caught a splendid fish.

As the course of the illness is not exactly without relevance for the amplification to be applied, we owe the reader a brief account of what happened. In the ten days following this initial dream the depression gradually eased, leading to complete recovery. The patient stayed in analysis with me for several months, and remained psychically sound to the end of his days.

A discussion of this dream appears in a later chapter. Here we amplify just one element, the trident. I must first mention that the patient, in his total apathy, was not capable of uttering one word about the dream, and all I felt I needed to say to him was that there seemed to be grounds for optimism for a speedy improvement in his condition.

With dream elements where the dreamer does not come up with any ideas of his own, although they play an important role in the dream, we then try, in accordance with Jung's teaching, to bring in objective material as a basis for comparison; in other words we try to amplify them.[17] The use of the trident as an article of fishing tackle certainly goes back to ancient times, and it is in fact still used today, e.g., in Sicily and in Provence, where it is called "foëne." The patient, however, being an extremely modern American, can hardly have been aware of this. I should also point out that in those days (1937) the popular sport of underwater fishing, with gun and trident, was not yet known. So the first association that comes to mind is the trident of Poseidon. When it comes to motifs of classical mythology, we can easily find the necessary parallel material to the books of K. Kerényi[18] or in the famous *Lexikon der griechischen und römischen Mythologie* by W. H. Roscher.[19] As we already know from Artemidor,[20] epiphanies of the Greek and Roman gods often occurred simply through the appearance of one of their attributes. In the Poseidon (Roman Neptune) myth, Zeus, Poseidon, Hades and Hera are the four children of Cronos and Rhea. Through the drawing of lots (*Iliad* XV, 189ff.), Zeus receives as his sphere of power the heavens, Poseidon the earth and the sea, and Hades the underworld.

1. Poseidon is first and foremost honored as the earth shaker, the one who calls forth earthquakes (ἐννοσίγαιος, ἐνοσίχθων, *ennosigaios, enosichthon* = earth shaker), but he is also the earth holder and husband of the earth (γαιήοχος *gaieochos* = earth mover) and Asphaleios (ἀσφάλειος) who provides security and stability (e.g., against earthquakes).

2. In the second place he is a storm god. The waves (sometimes referred to in English as white horses) and clouds are his storm-driven horses. The sea and wind demons obey him. He is highly emotional and has tempestuous love affairs with Gorgo, the Furies, Demeter and many others, apart from Amphitrite. A product of his union with Gorgo is Medusa, who in turn produces the *horses* Chrysaor and Pegasos (see 6 below).

3. As a sea god he is the Halios Geron, the Old Man of the Sea, and Nereus, Glaukos, Triton and Proteus all belong to him.

4. He is also the god of the inlands and inland waters, as well as the springs which come into being wherever he sticks his trident into the earth or, as a horse, strikes the earth with his hoof (Hippokrene). When there is a drought he provides water (rain) and ensures that it flows like the river Peneios in Thessalia. By driving in his trident he opens up valleys and navigable straits between seas, as with the Bosphorus and the Hellespont (for a positive meaning of earthquakes, see 1 above).

5. Poseidon is responsible for the growth of plants and hence is called Georgos (γεωργός, ploughing the earth and making it fertile)[21] or Phytalmios (φυτάλμιος, *phytalmios* = nourishing).

6. He is a horse tamer (cf. 2) and lord of the herds and horses and chariot races, and hence bears the name Hippios (ἵππιος). With his trident he created the first horse (Kolonos Hippios), and horses are sacrificed to him.

7. He is a birth, lineage and tutelary god of Man; in particular he is the divine tribal father of the Ionians (γενέθλιος, *genethlios* = tribal father).

8. Poseidon is also an oracle god (like all Chthonics). As such he owned Delphi before it went over to Apollo, and Pythia always called him first before the tripod.

9. He is also respected as a doctor (ἰατρός, *iatros*), e.g., on the island of Tenos, and he is the father of the two doctors from the Iliad, Machaon and Podaleirios.

His most important attributes are the tuna fish (Thynnos), the most useful fish in ancient times, and the trident, the Triaina (τρίαινα), lat. tridens. It is produced in the same way as the flashes of lightning of the Zeus Keraunios, in other words by the Cyclopes; it is his sceptre and signifies his dominion, his kingdom (as is also the case in India). This is beautifully represented in the West gable frieze of the Parthenon, where Poseidon is engaged in a dispute with Athena over his territorial rights. Of course, the trident also serves him as a weapon—against the giants, for example.

The Triaina is obviously a particularly phallic symbol. It should be pointed out that when we use the word "phallic," the meaning of the Greek φάλλος, the imitation of the male member, it is the symbol of the actual generative force of nature and the creative powers of Man, and it is certainly not a casual metaphor or euphemism for the word penis. Phallos is actually a pole made of fig or olive wood and is a cognate of the Latin *palus*, meaning pole. Its meaning is identical with that of the Indian Lingam. This accounts for the many productive characteristics of Poseidon, as listed in 1–9 above, and so it comes as no surprise when an earthquake or the appearance of Poseidon or his trident in a dream is regarded as a good omen in the dream book of Artemidorus.

In summing up we can say that Poseidon is one of the most powerful gods, that he embodies the chthonic side of the Olympus, that he is very irrational and emotional, and that when this leads to outbursts it also leads to something creative happening. (We are reminded here of the similar motif of the "reluctant creation" from the Calicapurana, first made accessible to us by Heinrich Zimmer.[22])

This outstanding creative power is now equivalent to the healing power[23] which, in mythological terms, produces health.

It is unlikely that our patient was familiar with the Poseidon mythology. In any case he was in such a pitiable state that he was not even able to make the obvious association between the trident and Neptune, despite the fact that the trident is actually the very impressive *deus ex machina* of his dream drama. Furthermore, we know retrospectively that the dream was heralding the immediate onset of the healing process. So it can only be either a case of a coinciding of dream and spontaneous remission of the depressive phase, or the appearance of a synchronistic phenomenon,[24] for a genuine causal link is extremely unlikely. But Poseidon has produced several such spontaneous effects with his lightning appearances, so that in this mythology, we are in exactly the same sphere as the dream, on the one hand, and the patient's real situation on the other.

This may be an example illustrating the concept put forward by Jung of an "arrangement" in the form of the divine attribute (trident = harmony of body-soul-spirit). In the perspective of the

24. February 1937   13. April 1937
New York   Zurich

Figure 1

dream at least it is a miracle cure, which can best be ascertained in
the two passport photographs (fig. 1, above) of the patient "before
and after the Poseidon epiphany." The rationally arguing psychiatrist will, of course, rest content with the well-known theory of
spontaneous remission with melancholy. But in doing so he does
not explain the dream, whereas we find it easier to accept the idea
of Poseidon intervening as Ἰατρός (*Iatros* = doctor), and we thus
lay ourselves open to the accusation of superstition. It would thus
be advisable for those in the psychiatric sphere to take dreams more
seriously and to pay careful attention to the frequency with which
coincidences occur in spontaneous remissions, irrespective of the fact
that even the most modern psychiatrist knows nothing about *how*
they come about.

Free Association versus Amplification

To depict the concept of amplification more precisely, we can contrast it with free association as applied by Freud.

In free association the dreamer is asked: "What springs to mind?"
in relation to a specific dream element a. We are given as an answer
the "free association" b. The next question is then about the associations with element b, which thus leads to a chain of elements
that are connected by association, as in the following schema:

$$a \text{-----} b \text{-----} c \text{-----} d \text{-----} \ldots\ldots x$$

If you play this game long enough, you will, under certain conditions, regularly land at the same *x*. For example, when I was a student in Paris I conducted the experiment with friends and acquaintances by taking as element *a* the inscription *"Defense d'afficher. Loi du 29 juillet 1881"* found everywhere there on the walls of public buildings, and having them make free associations with it. It didn't take long (in those years) until *x* had a sexual meaning. By making the --- an =, the circular meaning is made that *a* = *x*, and as *x* with Freud always refers to sexuality, then this is already expressed in *a*, q.e.d.!

As we can see, this way of drawing conclusions is not the recognition of something new but simply the return to the familiar, the ἀναγωγή (anagoge) of Aristotle, *a logical reductio in primam figuram*, and since Freud it is no secret that the prima figura = sexuality. This method is known as the chain or accumulation series, Sorites Syllogisticus (σωρός = accumulation), and the conclusion lies in the premise (*a* = *x*, therefore *x* = *a*). In other words the series of associations is interrupted when *x* has the meaning (sexual) expected in the theory. This procedure corresponds exactly to what is known in today's experimental psychology as "optional stopping." It is inadmissible, for any series of experiments must be carried out to the conclusion of the previously specified number of individual experiments, and cannot be arbitrarily interrupted when the person in charge of the experiment has the impression that he has collected a sufficient number of individual results which seem to confirm the working hypothesis or premise.

Further doubts about the infallibility of "free association" have even been expressed by Freudians themselves. For example, Judd Marmor[25-27] points out that Freud is content with the observation that this method "raises to a conscious level material that has been repressed and kept at bay by resistance."[28] But he goes on to ask what happens to that material that the patient was never conscious of, and which therefore cannot be repressed—in other words, material that is unconscious without being part of Freud's narrowly defined "unconscious." From a Jungian point of view, what springs to mind first and foremost here are the contents of the collective unconscious, which usually determine our behavior to a large extent, without our being conscious of them. Occasionally, however, they crop up as dream elements of a totally incomprehensible nature and can only be recognized as such and understood by means of amplification.

In the amplification process the object *a* is set as unknown or incomprehensible, and one carries on asking the question "What does that make you think of?'' until it becomes understandable, until its meaning is clarified. The question is a stereotype one: "What does *a* make you think of?", not b, c, etc. We do not associate in a linear fashion, as in free association, but concentrically to *a* and only to *a*. In this way *a* is augmented (amplified) until it has lost its fragmentary character and has become a complete picture. Along with Jung we have no qualms about contributing such material ourselves from our own fund of knowledge, especially from the spheres of mythology, fairy tales, folklore, etc. For in so doing, we remain in the same milieu as dreams, it being our conviction (a conviction shared by all depth psychology schools and corroborated by much experience) that dreams, myths, fairy tales, etc. not only have formal similarities but are in fact made of the same material. It is unfortunately true that a dangerous arbitrariness can creep in, but this danger can be reduced by adhering strictly to the schema of only introducing things that have indisputably objective links with *a*. Jung illustrated this as follows:

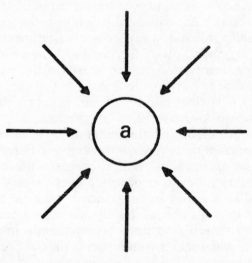

Figure 2

The impression must not be given that there are always such spectacular results as in the case described. They are, in fact, rare. Nor can the case itself be discussed here, as this would entail looking at a lengthy dream series and many other things (we shall come back to some of our patient's later dreams). Moreover, this is not the place to go into the Pilatus question of what is actually the *causa efficiens* in psychotherapy. The comments made above are intended solely as a typical example of amplification. Of course, the patient himself never learned about these amplifications, since I myself had to look them up in the corresponding literature. What cannot be denied is the fact that he had this initial dream and that this had an immediate effect, or, in more neutral terms, was followed by the healing process. There is no insisting on *post hoc ergo propter hoc*, but it should be clear that with the Poseidon mythology we are in the same sphere as the healing: impatient agitation which, with his state of total apathy, was something new and is very similar to Poseidon's well-known impetuosity (e-motion = moving out of lethargy) and the ensuing appearance of a phallic-creative (= healing) instrument with a happy outcome.

3. Experimental Methods

Attempts have also been made to make dreams more intelligible by trying to correlate the diverse nature of dreams with the different conditions under which the sleeping and dreaming took place, although it must be stated that these conditions can be manipulated in different ways.

(a) Dreams with Different Depths of Sleep

(1) Speculations of the Ancient Upanishads on Deep Sleep

In some of the ancient Upanishads there is extensive and interesting speculation about deep sleep, which they claim should be dreamless, for the atman is there (1) free from conception, (2) free from individuality, and (3) free from suffering. But he remains in existence (as in death, too) as the most important one, not subject to fatigue. He is the "hearer of hearing," the "seer of seeing," in other words the objectless subject of perception and recognition.

People in the western world have tried again and again to achieve this state, with the aid of every technique possible. Aldous Huxley felt he could use psychedelic drugs (mescalin, LSD, etc.) to open wide the "doors of perception." More recently this short cut seems to have made a deep impression on many of the younger generation.

As a consequence of conditions (1)–(3) above, the atman is pure and in a permanent state of "unmitigated bliss." In normal sleep he roams around, wanders about like the ψυχή (*psyche*) with the Greeks, and the dreams are the product of the experiences he acquires thereby. In deep sleep, however, the individual atman (or

purusha) is transformed by conditions (1)–(3) into the universal atman (or Brahman). This is when dreamless sleep is achieved, or this
is what it consists of. In Chand. Up. 6.8.1. it says: ". . . then he
(man) achieves unity with the Being One (the Brahman). He has
turned in on himself, that is why they say of him that he sleeps
(*svapiti*), for he has turned in on himself (*svam apita*)." (A *svami*
is one who is at one with himself.) This explains the famous Indian
belief that the embryo and the newborn child are all knowing. We
are instantly reminded of the fragment B89 of Heraclitus: τοῖς
ἐγρηγορόσιν ἕνα καὶ κοινὸν κόσμον εἶναι, τῶν δὲ κοιμωμένων ἕκαστον
εἰς ἴδιον ἀποστρέφεσθαι, i.e., "the awake have one single common
world, in sleep, each turns to his own."

From the above Indian theory there has developed a complete
yoga philosophy of release. For example, it says in the Maitr. Up.
6.25: "If someone, with his senses repressed as in sleep, is enabled
through the utter purity of his thoughts to gaze upon that sleepless,
ageless, deathless, sorrowless steersman, then he himself will become
that sleepless, ageless, deathless, sorrowless steersman." Betty
Heimann[29] makes the following comment:

> The aim of yoga technique is to achieve that which happens by it-
> self in deep sleep, namely to bring about the fading away of all ideas,
> wishes and the self, thus purging the atman. And in contrast to the
> original speculation about deep sleep, where, by its very nature, the
> fading away of ideas, like hearing, seeing, and so on was most strik-
> ingly prominent, as the fading away of psychological observation,
> yoga places the emphasis on the fading away of wishes, desires,
> passions.

In Buddhism this state is called nirvana, which corresponds to the
extinguishing of all thinking, desiring and suffering, and once again
is analogous to deep sleep.

In this context it strikes me as particularly interesting that as early
as 1846 J. E. Purkinje (1787–1869, Prag)[30] wrote:

> After the rotation of the usual time span of the exertions of being
> awake, of the psychic tension outwards, there arises an inclination
> toward returning to the subjectivity which is unaware of the concept
> of opposites, the tendency to sleep.

In this we see a fundamental idea similar to the Indian one.

Of course, this is not an experimental method in the sense of our
definition, but it is of interest when we consider the modern technical aids for sleep and dream research (see below), which is why
it is not out of place here, quite apart from its significance in the
history of human thought.

(2) Superficial Sleep

Everyone can observe that during light sleep dream images tend to crop up, i.e., more or less coherent series of pictures emerge, the elements of which consist of "remnants of the day." So the preoccupations of the conscious continue further into the dream world but are specifically modified in a dreamlike way. They, too, will appear in connected sequences which do not, or do not exactly, correspond to the waking or the real life situation. Our customary prejudices can also manifest themselves in such dream motifs. What most frequently appear reflected in such dreams are expectations of a pleasant or unpleasant nature, e.g., travel plans or examination fears. Moreover, I have frequently observed that patients coming to the psychiatrist for the first time have often dreamt that they have been to the dentist's (dreamlike modification of the psychiatrist, who, like a dentist, will be poking around).

At this point it should be made clear that the understanding of the different depths of sleep has become rather questionable, and has been greatly modified. This is discussed in a later section.

(b) Somatic Dreams

Our sensory organs do not switch off even in deep sleep, so that we still react to sense stimuli. However, the stimulus threshold is usually raised so that strong acoustic, optical or tactile signals are necessary. There is, of course, the famous "mother's sleep," during which the hearing threshold of women who have small children does not seem to be raised at all, so that they are awakened by the slightest whimper of their child. But this hearing is specifically for sounds made by the child, and, being a phenomenon of adjustment, is not a purely physiological but largely a psychological problem.

The latest investigations by Ian Oswald[31] have shown that out of a list of proper names played back at the same volume (decibels) from a tape recorder, the sleeper is awakened only by those that mean something to him (his own name, the name of his wife, etc.). Now if the signals generally remain below the waking threshold, they can then pass into the dream, having been processed in one way or another. Freud himself divided these stimuli up in logical form, and we adopt his system here as there is still no better way of putting it:

Where the enumeration of the dream sources is complete, there turn out to be four kinds, which are also used for the classification of the dreams:
1. External (objective) stimulation of the senses.
2. Internal (subjective) stimulation of the senses.

3. Internal (organic) physical stimuli.
4. Purely physical stimulus sources.[32]

External (Objective) Sense Stimuli

On the first kind of stimuli Freud quotes Jessen[33]:

"Any sound that is imperfectly perceived conjures up corresponding dream images—the rolling of thunder transports us into the thick
of battle, the crowing of a cock can be transformed into a human
cry of fear, the creaking of a door can lead to dreams of thieves
breaking in. If we lose our bedclothes during the night, we may
dream that we are going around naked or that we have fallen in the
water. If we lie in bed at an angle, with our feet hanging over the
side, we may dream that we are on the brink of a terrible abyss or
that we are falling down some steep hill. Should our head happen
to end up under the pillow, then there is a huge rock hanging over
us and is about to bury us. If semen accumulates, we have sensual
dreams, local pains give rise to the idea of maltreatment that has
been suffered, enemy attacks or physical injuries occurring. . ."

He then refers to Meier[34]:

Meier once dreamt that he had been attacked by people who laid him
on his back and drove a post into the ground between his big toe and
the one next to it. As he was imagining this going on in the dream,
he woke up and felt a straw stuck between his toes.

A. Maury[35] carried out a number of experiments on himself, or
had them carried out, and again Freud mentions some of them.

1. He is tickled on the lips and tip of his nose with a feather.—
He dreams of some terrible torture; a leech is placed on his face, then
torn off, taking the skin with it.
2. A pair of scissors is sharpened on some pincers.—He hears
bells ringing, then alarm bells and is transported back to June 1848.
3. He is made to smell eau de cologne.—He is in Cairo in the shop
of Johann Maria Farina. Then come wild adventures which he is unable to reproduce.
4. They pinch him in the back of the neck.—He dreams that they
are putting a plaster on a blister and thinks of a doctor who treated
him as a child.
8. A drop of water is placed on his brow.—He is in Italy, sweating profusely and drinking the white wine of Orvieto.[36]

Perhaps the most famous dream of all is Maury's dream of his
execution, which now follows in the exact wording[37]:

. . . one fact even more conclusive of the rapidity of dreams, a fact
which established to my mind that one instant is sufficient to produce

a long dream, is the following. I was a little indisposed, and was lying in my room, my mother by my side. I dreamt of the *Reign of
Terror*: I am witnessing scenes of massacre; I appear before the
revolutionary court. I see Robespierre, Marat, Fouquier-Tinville, all
the most villainous characters of that terrible period. I talk with
them. Finally, after many events which I can but imperfectly recall,
I am judged, condemned to death, and taken by cart into the middle
of an immense gathering in Revolution Plaza. I mount the scaffold,
the executioner ties me to the fatal board, he releases it, the blade
falls; I feel my head separate from my trunk. I awaken in the grips
of the most vivid anguish, and on my neck I feel the sash of my bed
which had suddenly detached itself, and had fallen on my cervical
vertebrae in the manner of a guillotine blade. All this had taken place
at that instant, as my mother confirmed, and yet it was that external sensation which I had taken as a point of departure for a dream
in which so many events had taken place one after another. At the
moment in which I was struck, the memory of that dreadful
machine, the effect of which the sash of my bed so well represented, had awakened all the imagery of an era in which the guillotine
had been the symbol.

Maury is a reputable scientist and acute observer, so his earlier
question about the possibility of lengthy dreams which seem to occur
in a short space of time should be taken seriously. Modern experimental dream research has voiced grave misgivings about this
time modification in dreams. This possibility has its limits, just as
with the investigations carried out by Schrötter described later in this
chapter. He had the test subjects state the beginning and end of the
dream in hypnosis. I would venture to express the opinion that so
far there have been no such cases in the laboratory, for there is a
considerable number of reports by people falling or drowning who
seem to have had very lengthy experiences, all in the space of a few
seconds—usually flashbacks of their whole lives.

Spitta[38] reports on a case of ether intoxication with an unmistak-
able expansion of the subjective sense of time. If there are ever psychologically oriented surgeons or dentists, the short narcosis would
probably be a fertile field for such investigations. Purkinje (p. 469,
note 30) has something interesting to say on the subject of the factor *t* in sleep and dream. On the basis of his experience, he says:

We should like to show more clearly the similarity between sleep
and death in the following psychological deduction of the concept.
When we wake up after a healthy, deep, dreamless sleep of 6 to 7
hours, and start to think about the time that has elapsed, we find that
for us the whole span of time can almost be reduced to one single
moment. Of course this moment, insofar as it is enclosed by other

moments in time, also belongs to the time we objectively recognize, but in its proximity with other unconscious moments in deep sleep, it is removed entirely from our awareness.

In the same way, in the state of sleep we lose all notion of space as well as every trace of awareness of the world and ourselves. The last mentioned is only regained when we wake up and, often only with difficulty, we latch onto recollections of the previous day. Imagine this state of unconsciousness lasting longer—days, weeks, months (as with those suffering from lethargy), then in this state more or less the same thing would happen as after one single night of deep sleep. The time spent asleep, no matter how long it lasted, would just have had the time span of one second. So one could say: during every period of sleep, be it long or short, the soul retreats into the eternity of its being, into a state which recognizes neither space nor time; it gives up its outward appearance, which is conditioned by sensuality, yet without breaking off completely the link with material existence, which it in fact resumes on waking with greater reciprocal action, for the organic individuality of the body has continued to exist during sleep, and has never ceased to maintain all the conditions of the inner relationship and renewal in uninterrupted identity.

In death only one aspect of these processes seems to present itself. The soul retreats into the eternity of its being, losing all consciousness and conception of time and space with their sensory content. By way of contrast, the living connection to the hitherto organic individuality, the body, seems to be completely destroyed, for it begins to decompose and return to the common elements of the earth. Thus there can be no reestablishing of consciousness in the same body, and death would, in the commonly held view, put an end to all existence of the soul as we know it.

Premature as it might be to deny the sleeping soul the possibility of the next ensuing awakening, it would be just as premature to do so with the soul asleep in death. This logical conclusion derives from the natural preconception that the existence of the soul must never be seen other than together with the body and secured by it; and if one wishes to pursue this line, one would seek for it a place in the brain, if possible in the smallest compartment, actually in one single point. Yet the real seat of the soul can only be the eternal, timeless, spaceless mental being itself, from which it only gives the appearance of emerging into the confines of the finiteness of the relationship to the world, and into which being the way back is always open and in actual fact can never be blocked.

The famous story of the night journey of the prophet Mohammed is very amusing because of its rationalistic "proof" and the ensuing experimental confirmation: according to the version that has been handed down, Mohammed is said to have held 70,000 talks with God in the course of one night journey and on his return to have found his bed still warm and some water still running out of a jug he had knocked over in his hasty departure. The story goes on that the Sultan of Egypt is said to have objected to this expansion of time and so refused to believe the story. The sheikh, however, won him over by having him submerge himself in the bathtub and then bring his head out at once. In those few seconds the Sultan has a whole series of sad and joyful experiences: he is destitute and cast ashore on some foreign shore, then he finds a beautiful and wealthy wife, has 7 sons and 7 daughters by her, becomes poor again in the end, and as he comes up for air realizes that it was all a momentary illusion.[39]

We find similar things in many Christian legends of saints. Whereas in such cases subjective time expands, there is also the opposite manifestation of the contraction of subjective time, a motif that is typical of a whole cycle of legends. The most well-known one is probably the legend of the seven sleepers: because of the persecution of the Christians by the Emperor Decius (251 A.D.) seven brothers hid in a cave by Ephesus, fell asleep there and were walled in. In the year 446 (under Theodosius II), the cave was opened, quite by chance. The young men woke up (the 195 years are contracted more or less into one night), surrounded by the aura of saintliness, had the miracle confirmed by Bishop Martin and the Emperor, then died. One is reminded here of the Kyffhäuser legend of the Hohenstaufen Emperor Barbarossa.

Also notorious are the fakirs who have themselves walled up for long periods. If ever such a case should happen under scientifically sound conditions, we would be in the sphere of parapsychology, where if we accept telepathy, clairvoyance, precognition and psychokinetics, the space-time coordinates seem to behave in a similarly odd fashion.

The Norwegian professor of philosophy John Mourly Vold (1850–1907),[40] who moved on from Hegel to Kant's Criticism, worked painstakingly on thousands of experiments to study the influence of objective sense stimuli on dreams, and came up with a postulate of causal dependency. They were almost always experiments on himself; in systematic fashion he conducted stimulus tests on almost every part of his body. Vold's thoroughness is shown by these two experiments. In the first he placed pieces of wood in his bed or fastened them to a part of his body and then observed his dreams.

On the morning of February 11, when the pieces of wood lay rather high up on one side, I had a restless dream with many different aspects to it.

Dream:
(a) With others I am a spectator at a sort of show; a gentleman sitting next to me keeps nudging me in the ribs, either to draw my attention to something or to start a quarrel.
(b) Out of my sleeve I draw some animals, which look like large spiders.

Analysis:
The pressing of the pieces of wood on the side is seen as a sequence of brief, successive thrusts, and together with a theme from daily life (a show), is worked into a short scene. The perception of the pressure from the side seems to be less precisely located, probably as a result of a feeling of slight pressure from clothes at the same point (which was later observed to be the case). The same rhythm in the sensing of pressure (the pressing of animals and removal of same).

Afterwards I usually had the pieces of wood at my side, but not attached to me, so that any pressure on the back or the side would only arise by chance. Then on the evening of the 22nd I fastened them to my back again. At the same time I wound a thread of wool round one of the fingers on my left hand and placed some lather mixed with coffee beans under my nose. The smell did not lead to any dreams and I did not repeat the second part of the experiment; the results from wrapping wool round my finger I dealt with earlier as finger experiments; there remain one or two factors relating to the pressure on the back.

Dream:
(a) I am making my way to a station with the lady from dream 1 in order to go for a ride on the train.

Analysis:
What is interesting here is that in returning to the first form of the experiment, the first motif of dream 1 is the first one to reappear: train journey with the anxious lady. But the motif is not as strong here: instead of the jolting of the railway compartment there is just the notion of the train ride and the notion of the station.

| (b) I can see a large animal with one or two humps on its back; a man seems to be sitting on the animal's back. | The back with the pieces of wood is perceived very clearly here, but objectified and transformed into an animal with humps (number rather vague); the man represents a frequency of the representation of the pressure. |

According to Freud,[41] Vold summed up his conclusions as follows:

1. The position of a limb in the dream more or less corresponds to reality, i.e., one dreams about a static state of the limb which corresponds to the real one.

2. If one dreams about the movement of a limb, it is always the case that one of the positions that occurs during that movement corresponds to reality.

3. One can attribute to a third party the position of one's own limb in a dream.

4. One can also dream that the movement is impeded.

5. The limb in a certain position can appear in the dream as an animal or a monster, and there will be a certain similarity between the two.

6. The position of a limb can give rise to thoughts in the dream which have some connection with this limb. For example, doing things with fingers makes one dream of counting.

Let us recall here that the original Greek word for "counting" is πεμπάζω (pempazo), i.e., counting on five fingers.

Reading Vold's two volumes, the modern psychologist is struck by the unfailing regularity with which the author dreamt and how unfailingly his dreams fitted in with the experimental setup, so that the effect of autosuggestion is bound to cross his mind. Vold, however, steered clear of this aspect of a causal relationship.

Internal (Subjective) Stimulation of the Senses

It is not really clear what is meant by these stimuli. It seems to me that they are a relic of Aristotle's "vibrations" (see below). But people compare them to entoptic manifestations, buzzing in the ears, and so on—in other words to endosomatic stimulations. Because such sensations can hardly be objectified, it is difficult to establish a possible connection with dream motifs. In Freud's opinion,[42] these manifestations are not so much dreams as rather so-called hypnagogic visions (from the Greek ὕπνος (hypnos) = sleep, and ἀγωγός (agogos) = leading to, inducing). These are the fleeting, constantly changing, hardly coherent visual impressions which many people tend to have just before falling asleep. Maury also made a study of them, and his experience was summed up by Freud[43] as follows:

They do not appear unless there is a certain emotional passiveness, a falling off in attentiveness. But all it needs is just one second of such lethargy for anyone to see a hypnagogic hallucination, after which one may wake up again, and experience the whole thing several times before finally falling asleep. If one wakes up not too long afterwards, one often succeeds, according to Maury, in proving that the same images appeared in the dream as in the hypnagogic hallucination just before falling asleep. This happened to Maury once with a series of grotesque figures with distorted features and weird hairstyles, which plagued him with incredible insistency in the period before falling asleep and which he remembered dreaming about after waking up. On another occasion, just as he was experiencing hunger pangs because he had put himself on a meager diet, he had a hypnagogic vision of a dish and a hand with a fork in it which was taking some food from the dish. In the dream he was at an abundantly laid table and could hear the noise that the diners were making with their forks. Another time, when he fell asleep with his eyes irritated and painful, he had the hypnagogic hallucination of microscopically small signs which he had to decipher one by one with great difficulty; on being woken after an hour of sleep, he remembered a dream in which there appeared an open book with very small letters which he had to plough his way through.

The physiologist Johannes Müller also dealt at great length with hypnagogic visions in his work *Uber die phantastischen Gesichtserscheinungen*,[44] which is still worth reading today. Moreover, the famous Yale professor George Trumbull Ladd, whose textbook *Psychology* (London, 1894) was a standard work for a long time, also picked up the subject of visions in a work entitled "Contribution to the Psychology of Visual Dreams."[45] Freud sums up Ladd's observations as follows:

Ladd perfected the habit of waking himself up abruptly, without opening his eyes, two to five minutes after falling asleep. He then had the opportunity to compare his retina sensations, just as they vanished, with the dream images still in his memory. He assures us that on each occasion there was a close link between the two in that the radiant points and lines of the retina's own light, the contour drawing, as it were, provided the schema for the psychically perceived dream figures. For example, an arrangement of the radiant points in the retina in parallel lines corresponded to a dream in which he could see clearly printed lines, which he read and studied. To use his own words: The clearly printed side, which he had read in the dream, dissolved into an object that appeared to his waking perception like a piece of a genuine printed page which one looks at from a great distance through a little hole in a piece of paper, to pick out something clearly. Ladd claims, without underestimating the central part of the phenomenon, that there is hardly a visual dream we have that did not depend on the material of the internal state of stimulation of the retina. This applies particularly to dreams that occur just after one has fallen asleep in a dark room; whereas for morning dreams, just before waking, the stimulation source is the objective light pouring into the eye in the room which is no longer dark.

So both authors start out from the stimulations of the retina resounding from the waking state and from the nervus opticus, the remnants of which are said to be incorporated into the ensuing dreams. So in this respect they are of the same opinion as Aristotle (see below).

In recent times Herbert Silberer has tackled the subject again from a more psychological point of view.[46] He is particularly interested in how the change in the state of consciousness (sleep-waking) on falling asleep or waking up (hypnagogic and hypnopomic visions) is represented in images. He compares this changing from one state to another with the crossing of a threshold, and thus speaks of *threshold symbolism*. In the work referred to he sums up his conclusions as follows:

> The symbolism of waking up (and falling asleep) makes use of those images in which the dominant feature is a change of situation, a transition or decline, the crossing of a threshold. In such representations the image of the threshold itself (as a door threshold) is often used, as is crossing a stretch of water, diving into water, sinking, and so on, being disturbed, joining and separating, departing and arriving, saying goodbye and hello, opening and closing, and similar actions and situations.[47]

Under the title "Die Halluzination im Halbschlaf" he returns to the subject in 1919 in his book *Der Traum*[48] and describes a hypnagogic vision:

> I am lying in bed almost asleep. Some thought is on my mind. Sleepiness gradually gains the upper hand, my mind becomes blurred, my train of thought loses the thread. Suddenly, instead of the thought on my mind there is in front of me, as if by magic, an image, three-dimensional, so real you can reach out and touch it. Instead of "image" it would be more accurate if I said: a "reality," a scene that I experience as reality. The liveliness of the face surprises

me, shakes me out of the sleep that I was on the brink of. I am wide awake again and realize that what I have just experienced, i.e., the hypnagogic vision, is a pictorial expression of that very thought that I had lost as sleep took hold of me. Because of my fatigue, tiring abstract thinking had suddenly been replaced by a less tiring, pictorial viewing. "Viewing" in the broadest sense of the term, for the hallucination is not purely optical, but, like the dream, so distributed over the various sensory spheres that we feel the whole as a reality into which we have been transported with our whole being. The facial features make the strongest impression, which is not surprising, given their overriding importance. To make the process perfectly clear, I shall give some examples:

1. Example.—Conditions: Lying in bed at night I am thinking about the fact that in an essay that I am writing there is one part that I shall have to improve. As I am considering this I am overcome by sleep and the following hallucinated *scene* appears: I am busy planing a piece of wood smooth. Immediately I wake up again and try to justify or *interpret*: Planing the wood smooth is an image for what I was planning to do; it corresponds to polishing up the clumsy part of my essay.

15. Example.—Conditions: I am lying clothed on a sofa and, in accordance with my need for sleep, am about to remove myself from the state of being awake (after a previous short sleep).—*Scene*: I am putting on a coat (accompanied or being collected by someone), as if to leave.—*Interpretation*: Sleep appears here as a person who comes to collect me. The "leaving" reflects the removal from the state of being awake. The coat recalls the covering or cloaking of clear consciousness. It plays the same role as the covering cloud in various myths which is to be seen as a symbol of removal. Anyone wishing to be in a state of being spiritually removed must, according to certain rites, wrap a cloak round himself.

16. Example.—Conditions: I am woken in the morning at the usual time. As I have nothing urgent to attend to and still feel sleepy, I decide to sleep a little longer.—*Scene*: I am setting about leasing out something (not defined) to someone.—*Interpretation*: In the idea of leasing out there is the idea of handing over. I am handing myself over or yielding to sleep. There is also partly the idea of release from the worry of administration. The notion of the well-ordered psychic process as a household that is administered, is not actually so farfetched.

The fact that Silberer describes these "translations" of his own psychic conditions into optical images is merely disguised egocentricity and therefore not a suitable expression. As will emerge from later remarks, body semantics would be a more appropriate term.

Internal (Organic) Stimuli

It is a popular superstition that dreams (especially unpleasant ones) come "from the stomach" or from the adopting of a particular sleeping position. The view is equally ingrained that if we are hungry we dream of food, and that if we are thirsty we dream of drink, a view that seems to be confirmed by the Roman proverb "*canis panem somniat, piscator pisces.*" The latest experimental investigations, however, seem to disprove these theories.

As early as 1874, the Leipzig philosophy and pedagogics professor and Herbart student Ludwig Strümpell (1812–1899) had carried out the examination of the influence of physical factors on dream variables. In his book *Die Natur und Entstehung der Träume* he states[49]:

> In sleep the soul achieves a much deeper and broader consciousness of perception of its physicality than when awake. Hence it is compelled to receive certain stimulus impressions and let them take their effect, impressions that come from parts of the body and changes in the body about which it knew nothing when awake.

Freud studied the literature on the subject and gives the following extract:

> Disturbances of the internal organs seem to trigger off dreams in quite a number of people. The commonest example cited is the frequency of nightmares in people suffering from heart or lung illnesses. . . . The dreams of heart patients are usually short and end with waking up in terror; they almost always involve death in terrible circumstances. Lung patients dream about suffocating, jostling crowds, fleeing, and a striking number of them feature the common nightmare. . . . With digestive disturbances the dream contains features from the area of pleasure and disgust. Finally, the influence of sexual stimulation on the content of the dream is part of everyone's experience, and provides the strongest support for the whole theory of dreams being triggered off by stimulation of the organs.[50]

Even more convincing evidence is the occurrence of fire in the dreams of patients with inflammation. But here, too, unfortunately, we do not have the statistical material called for at the outset. On the other hand, even Aristotle talks about these links, and later such experienced doctors as Hippocrates and Galen made diagnostic use of such dream motifs (see below). Once again it can be seen here, as in so many other questions in dream research, that if they are to be solved it would be advantageous to start out from extreme, i.e., from pathological, conditions.

Purely Physical Stimulus Sources

Strictly speaking, of course, they do not come under our section (b), but are associated with it in that they lead to the discussion of the ensuing methods, which all experiment with physical "stimuli."

KARL SCHRÖTTER

Karl Schrötter reported on "experimental dreams" in 1912 in the *Zentralblatt für Psychoanalyse*,[51] experiments in which he made use of

(a) *Physical Stimuli in Combination with Hypnosis.*

Schrötter's experiment conditions are the following:

> For the purpose of the experiment the test people were put into a deep hypnotic trance, the features of which, as is commonly known, are a total lack of consciousness and subsequent amnesia. I then gave them appropriate dream suggestions. After about 4–5 minutes the subjects spontaneously began dreaming. Following my instructions they indicated the beginning and end of the dream by certain movements, so that the duration of the conscious dream process could be measured precisely. After they woke up, they gave the content of the dream. In another series of experiments the subjects dreamed in the night following the evening of the experiment. In these cases, once again as a result of posthypnotic suggestion, the dreams of the test subjects were written down in the morning and handed to me.
>   I tackled the second group quite independently, on the basis of the Freudian attitude to the problem. A latent dream content, similar to the one discovered by Freud and his school through their method of dream analysis, is used as a dream suggestion. The technique of the experiment is the same as in Group 1. It must be stated specifically that the test subjects did not know Freud's research and had no idea about the meaning of their dreams.[52]

From the following examples, the reader may see how suggestion and physical stimulation can affect dreams:

> 9. Experiment. Test subject Mrs. E. *Suggestion*: Dream about something that symbolizes your present psychic condition. *Dream* (under hypnosis): I am walking through a wood with the leaves in autumnal colors. Then the path starts to slope up; it is cold and icy. There is someone walking alongside me but I can't see who it is; but I can feel the pressure of a hand; then I feel very thirsty. There is a spring babbling nearby. I want to drink from it but above it is a sign like the one on bottles of poison—the skull and crossbones.

Comment: The dream reflects the unhappy mood of the test subject when she learnt that Lieutenant H. had syphilis.

12. Experiment. Test subject Mr. Fr. *Suggestion*: You have a toothache and a slight urge to pass water. In the course of five minutes you will have a dream. *Dream*: We were at the Watschenmann in the Prater fairground in Vienna. I kept hitting him till his face grew bigger and bigger. Then we went off to a pub in a boat, where we drank a lot. *Duration of dream*: 1 minute, 20 seconds. *Comment*: The symbolism of the boating is clear. The conclusion gives the motivation for the urge to pass water.[53]

Unfortunately Schrötter's fourteen experiments are not enough for us to be able to draw conclusions. What is of interest, however, is his method of specifying the duration of the dream. But even here he unfortunately only gives five specifications, which range from 1 minute, 20 seconds to 4 minutes, 5 seconds, although it can be said roughly that the shortest dream text corresponds to the shortest dream time, and the longest text to the longest dream time. Today these figures are arrived at with the aid of an oculogram, and judging from our experiences in the laboratory, they seem to be similar to those of Schrötter. It is, of course, difficult to judge whether the length of the text corresponds in a linear way to the duration of the dream. So far we have the impression that the test subject himself can calculate very well the duration of the dream phases, but one must bear in mind the experience of Maury quoted above.

KARL ALBERT SCHERNER

Also of interest is the fact, based on experiments, that as in experiment 9 above, a feeling or mood can be translated into a graphic picture (autumnal wood, cold and icy, poison). At that time, the word "symbolism" was used by Freud and others. In reality, however, it is simply a language of allegory, dealt with particularly by Karl Albert Scherner in his book *Das Leben des Traumes*.[54] He comes to the conclusion that the dream translates the organ stimulation so regularly into allegorical language that it is possible to set up a key for this symbolism. The following excerpts will serve as examples:

1. Any sullen mood is lacking in harmony and so calls for unpleasant images and provokes restless emotions and movements. An elderly lady with a violent temper, who often gets annoyed and having had a real outburst one day, had the following dream that night: With a young lady she could not stand in real life she was walking out of the town into the country to attend to some domestic matter.

They come to a farmhouse on the roof of which three cats are sitting, as large again as ordinary cats, their legs stretched wide apart; there are five more cats pushing around wildly. All of a sudden one of the cats jumps off the roof onto the back of the lady accompanying her (the unpopular one); she takes fright of course. . . .[55]

2. The general designation of the fantasy for the human body is: a building of walls, tiles and beams, in other words, what we call a "house." It is obvious that by choosing this symbol for the body, the fantasy is giving an apt description of the organic structure of the body which, like the building of walls and tiles, has its architecture and also a number of cavities and chambers. . . .[56]

3. If it is a representation of the inner mouth cavity, which is particularly the case with tooth irritation dreams, where the whole surroundings of the picture falls down, then the fantasy usually selects the vaulted rooms of the house, e.g., a high vaulted entrance hall or dining room, and it often depicts, from the vaulted hall the cellar steps at the side, to convey the passage of the gullet.[57]

4. . . . thus the image of the flame when there is a face irritation shows the energizing light fluid of the internal powers of sight (before waking up); the roaring current of air and the crackling flame in the lung irritation dream depict the air for breathing and the combustion process in the lungs themselves; the foaming flood of water indicates the water accumulating in the bladder.[58]

5. For example, in bladder irritation dreams we see inflated bags and suchlike floating on water or we are at the water's edge in a garden where we are admiring the splendid pumpkins; pumpkins and bags represent the shape of the bladder.[59]

6. Should there be one single room to represent the body, particularly beloved by the fantasy in cases of headaches, then the ceiling of the room represents the head height of the body and the headache is depicted in the form of horrifying spiders or some sort of threatening monster on or by means of the ceiling of the room.[60]

7. A lady with a severe headache dreamt she was in a room of a house known to her; the whole ceiling was covered with cobwebs, and in them were spiders as large and as repulsive as toads; they were all piled up in the corners of the ceiling and kept crossing the wall.[61]

8. But ultimately the fantasy observes the law generally valid in all symbolic dream formations starting from specific nerve stimuli. According to this law, at the beginning of the dream the fantasy only paints the stimulus object in the most remote and freest allusions, but at the end, when the outburst of painting has exhausted itself, paints the stimulus itself or the organ concerned, or openly exposes its function; at this point the dream, itself depicting its organic cause, reaches its end.[62]

It can be seen clearly from the above how an intuition which in itself is correct can be carried to absurdity if one aspect of the matter is exaggerated. It is our opinion that the author jumps to conclusions about the somatic cause of such images, completely overlooking the fact that such allegorical language is better left on the purely psychological level. The popular superstition that dreams come from the stomach can be translated back to the purely psychic fact that there is something going on that "one cannot swallow" or "not digest." This point of view also provides a better understanding of the fact that when in dreams there is, for example, anxiety (from the Latin *angustia* = tightness), then "wicked men" appear, and with a violent affect there are "wild animals." But of course anxiety and affects have an influence in turn on the physical sphere, which takes us back to the old psycho-physical problem, about which there is more in the first volume of this textbook.

Such psycho-physical correspondences have always raised the question of the abode of the soul, and since time immemorial there have been fully fledged systems of "body symbolism," ascribing specific psychic characteristics or qualities to the various organs and parts of the body.

It is Indian and Chinese medicine that have pursued this idea furthest, and, of course, yoga. One only needs to compare the Tantra yoga or the Chinese treatise on "The Golden Flower." But these systems have also permeated the West. Such figures of speech as "I can't stomach the thought" or "His heart missed a beat," and many more, are evidence of the fact that people have always made these connections. The Böhme students Graber and Gichtel[63] dealt with these questions systematically, and what is striking is that there are marked similarities with tantric concepts, yet a tradition or migration hardly seems feasible (cf. fig. 3).

In the Jewish sphere, Tobia Nerol (Tobias Cohn or Tobia Kohen b. Jirmijja Moses Nerol), in his encyclopedia *Sepher Haolamoth*,[64] compared man's body to a house in which the soul dwells and localizes the corresponding physiological and psychological functions (cf. fig. 4). Ottavio Scarlatini (Bologna 1684),[65] who sees the human body as an "inhabited temple," describes with great differentiation the soul representatives of the parts of the body and the organs.

German figures of speech also compare man to a house, the house of the soul, as for example in *"er ist ein gemütliches Haus,"* (he is a good-natured house), *"es brennt bei ihm im oberen Stübli,"* (it is burning in his attic), etc. But our ancient medicine also operated with such assumptions, as shown, for example, by the bloodletting man or the zodiac signs, which, as Melotheses (the positioning of the limbs), give the correct composition of body and soul. Furthermore, in the event of an error (illness) they also indicate where the

Figure 3
First illustration in Graber and Gichtel, representing the condition of
"natural man" (after Adam's fall)

Figure 4
This picture in Tobias Cohn is intended to represent the correspondences
between the organs and functions of the human body and the installations
in a house

leeches, cupping instruments or phlebotomies are to be located. This then leads on to astrological medicine and to the concept of the cosmic correspondence between macro- and microcosmos (cf. fig. 5).

(b) *Physical Stimuli in Combination with the Association Experiment*.

The idea of setting up specific physical stimuli, establishing what the reaction is and comparing these reactions with the test subject's dreams at the time was first conceived by Jung in his work on "Association, Dream and Hysterical Symptom."[66] Reference has already been made to this in Volume I of this textbook,[67] and at this point will just be dealt with in reference to the relationship between the two factors of Association and Dream. This relation is actually a keystone for Jung's theoretical concept of the dream: it emerged

FIGURE 5. Bloodletting man. He represents the connections said to exist between parts of the body and organs and signs of the zodiac.

here for the first time that the disturbances in the Association Experiment formed around the same contents as the contents of the dreams. As we know, disturbances are simply transliterations of complexes, and thus the dream is a channel for the complexes to be acted out. To a certain extent the complexes are personified in the dreams.

Unfortunately that is as far as it went, so that there is no large supply of easily accessible material and hence the theory lacks statistical confirmation. In practice, however, we have this concept confirmed day in and day out.

In the literary field this theory led to a violent dispute over the role of the complex, the controversy being particularly heated over the question of whether the complex should be regarded as the actual *causa morbi*. Today the dispute strikes us as somewhat naive and can only be accounted for by the thirst for knowledge of the authors at the time.

The links between the effects of complexes in the Association Experiment and in the dream are as relevant as ever for the theory of dreaming, and could, as stated earlier, be given over to statistical processing. But it is striking, as we mentioned at the beginning, that the people professionally involved with dream interpretation seem to feel no need whatsoever to create a reliable foundation for their "science."

(c) *Silberer's Lecanomantic Method.*

The only author to have pursued the ideas in Jung's "Diagnostic Association Studies" and to have developed them in an imaginative way is Herbert Silberer. He uses the same parameters as Jung, i.e., association and dream, but introduces a third dimension, the so-called "lecanomantic observing." He is thus picking up on a method which was widespread in the ancient world for the purpose of fortune telling: One sat down in front of a λεκάνη (*lekane* = large bowl, tub) filled with a liquid, placed lights round it and sought inspiration in the light reflections on the surface of the liquid. The λεκανομάντεια (*lekanomanteia*) is thus the forerunner of what is still common today as crystal gazing. Silberer worked for years with this method and had a large number of talented test subjects. He had all his studies published in the *Zentralblatt für Psychoanalyse.*[68] We give one of his examples here (X. Experiment) which shows that Silberer was a forerunner of Jung in that the method is clearly identical with that of "active imagination" as introduced by Jung later.[69]

X. Experiment

Section I. Scene 1: I see the black cat with the glowing circle.

Section II. Scene 2: I see the old Jew. He is praying, praying in front of a pulpit. . . .

Scene 3: . . . from there someone passes a Bible down to him but he does not reach for it; it is passed down lower and lower but he backs away and does not want it.

Scene 4: He strokes his hair . . .

Scene 5: . . . and becomes a little child.

Scene 6: . . . the Bible turns into a little child.

Scene 7: they approach each other and kiss . . . etc.

Scene 8: The hand that held the Bible rests over them and blesses them.

Section III. Scene 9: I can see a black coffin and lights round it. Doves fly out of the coffin.—Down below I can see the old Jew. He is weeping and says that he is buried himself and has to look at his own grave.

Scene 10: He refuses to answer and threatens me with his hand when I ask him.

Scene 11: ('He has to be consoled!') He turns into a white cloud. Another (white cloud) comes toward him. They touch each other.

Scene 12: Once again I asked the old Jew (who he was); he replies that he is part of me and that I should know that.

Scene 13: Monks are creeping behind the coffin as if out of a cave.

Scene 14: They want to carry the coffin away, but they cannot.

Section IV. Scene 15: The coffin has disappeared and in its place there is a woman, a very large one; she has a face at the front and the back. On her head there is a cloud with two wings. Both faces are puffed up. One face speaks. She asks why she has wings when the other face won't let her fly.

Scene 16: The wings press in on her and she gets smaller and smaller.[70]

By comparing such processes with the results of the Association Experiment conducted at the same time and with the dreams that occurred then; Silberer reached some remarkable conclusions:

1. Figures appear that keep coming back, so that he speaks of *types*. But they can undergo metamorphoses (Jung would speak of archetypal figures).

2. At the beginning there are individual scenes, interrupted by breaks. Later these gaps are filled with the result that the process hangs together more, as in a dream.

3. The number of scenes also increases at the same time.

4. It is then possible to get into conversation with the "types."

5. The associations are not based on visions; they are not subor-

dinated to them, but are based just as much on complexes as on visions and are coordinated with them. Visions and associations take turns to reinforce their interpretations by both pointing concentrically to the same complex groups.

6. The figures (types) are physical powers which develop, and their game illustrates the game of the soul's powers, i.e., becomes more and more the symbolism of the "functional categories." What Silberer means here are the self-illustrations of the psychic structure and their dynamics, and he contrasts them with the "material categories," which are simply illustrations of contents. The "functional categories" with him correspond to an "internalization," about which he says:

> What one probably has to imagine in the process of internalizing the significance of a figure is roughly as follows: The figure first appears in the service of an episode where the stress is on the affect (starting from a complex). It remains in contact with the relevant complex and forges new links with related complexes. Every time it is utilized, something new clings to the figure and brings it new life, thereby intensifying it. Thus the figure lands in the middle of a large circle of meaning; it represents what is common to all the episodes attached to it; it becomes a type.[71]

It is clear that the distinction that Silberer makes is what Jung introduced later, and more clearly, as the interpretation of a dream element on the objective level (material category) and on the subjective level (functional category).

As regards the general discussion on the experimental methods, it must be said that none of them is in a position to indicate a purely causal link between the stimuli and the dreams that occur at that time or later. Either there is (1) a sort of *translation factor* between them or then (2) the whole experimental system is more coincidental and there is an *autonomous factor* at work.

This also means that in both cases the dream still calls for an *interpretation* and that the ancient oneiromancy is thus legitimately justified. It was described by the ancients as a μάντική ἄτεχνος, *mantike atechnos* (a practice based solely on the divine revelationary nature of the soul itself), in contrast to a μάντική ἔντεχνος (*mantike entechnos*), based on longer observation of the processes (of nature), and probably only a few exceptionally talented people succeeded with it, although we would like to turn it into a *mantike entechnos*. However, let us never forget the various fundamental difficulties discussed above, for they remain with us even when the most up-to-date technical aids are brought in.

The efforts to relate the dream more closely to the body have multiplied over the past 10 years. After the discovery of Aserinsky (see below), dozens of laboratories were set up where work goes on all night all over the world, to research the physiology and psychology of dreaming in totally new ways. The results are not yet fruitful, but everyone knows that in research, success only comes with a great deal of patience and unflagging enthusiasm. So I would like to conclude this chapter with at least a few thoughts that can and should be expressed about this biology and psychology of dreaming from the Jungian point of view.

4. Modern Experimental Approaches to the Dream

It is common knowledge that the dream as custodian of sleep was Freud's first working hypothesis. It corresponds to his then neo-lamarckian biological point of view and actually has little to do with psychology. There is a more psychological concept in his second hypothesis that all dreams are connected with wish fulfillment, which then logically led to the idea of a censor. Jung did not believe in the censor but assumed that the dream stated what it had to say in a very uninhibited fashion, just as the Talmud describes the dream as its own interpretation, and then of course the additional acceptance of a censor function is superfluous.

On the other hand, modern experimental findings pose the question once again; we know today that without exception we all dream several times a night, even if we wake up in the morning convinced that we have been "happily free of dreams" in our sleep. One wonders whether on these many occasions the "censor" has succeeded in simply blocking out all recollections of dreams, which makes it a memory factor, thus making the discussion even more complicated. This and many other questions concerning dreams have now come into the sphere of scientific verifiability, now that we have come across newly discovered neurophysiological characteristics of sleep. Speaking purely scientifically, it must be said that it is hardly possible to understand the dream without a better knowledge of its natural prerequisite—sleep. And we will hardly understand sleep without a better knowledge of waking and consciousness. Consciousness will be dealt with more thoroughly in Vol. III of this textbook, but we must take a closer look at sleep here, for *hypnos* ("Υπνος = sleep) and *oneiros* ("Ονειρος = dream) are inseparable brothers even back in Greek mythology, children of the night (*Νύξ, nyx*). They are also very powerful (*πανδαμάτωρ, panda-*

mator, Il. XIV) rulers over all gods and people, for even the gods are under them. (With the Greeks the gods sleep and dream, too!)

What follows next are the most important neurophysiological findings relevant to the understanding of sleep and dream:

Important findings about sleep are due first and foremost to the technique of the electroencephalograph (EEG), introduced in 1929 by Hans Berger (Jena). This is a recording of rhythmic, electrical potential fluctuations, which can be conducted away from the scalp and which are related to brain activity. The waking EEG is very different from the sleeping EEG, and in the latter it has been possible since Loomis (1937) to distinguish five different phases. Later W. Dement rationally reduced them to four (phases I to IV, from light to deep sleep). But after the observations of Aserinsky and Kleitman, it became necessary to introduce another phase of sleeping EEG, one which is very different from all the other sleep phases and, moreover, is accompanied by a second phenomenon—rapid, conjugated eye movements of the sleeper (under closed lids). Since Dement termed this phase Rapid Eye Movement sleep it has become known purely and simply as REM sleep. The phenomenon is a remarkable one in many ways, and remains barely understood; at any rate all the explanations put forward so far have been inadequate. (Which is why is has just as many names as the philosophers' stone, which is also an unknown quantity.) What is of greatest interest to us is that it occurs fairly regularly about every 90 minutes a night. Looking at the eye movements, the researchers had the idea that there might be a connection between this phase and dreaming. Now that the REM-EEG and the eye movements are so well defined, one has the opportunity to wake the sleeper in or after a REM phase (REMP) and ask him whether he has been dreaming.

Many thousands of such tests have shown that in 80 percent of those cases the test subjects really do state that they have just been dreaming. With the same test in a non-REM-phase (NREMP), the reply is only positive in fewer than 20 percent of the cases, which points to a very high correlation for REM/dream. What is also convincing is the fact that the subjectively estimated length of the dream (or the objective dream text) correlates positively with the length of the REMP, which, as we have mentioned, seems to contradict Maury.

This experimental set-up has made it possible to objectivize a number of factors about dreaming. Experiments have been conducted to find out whether it is possible to verify a direct correlation between the state of the body and the contents of the dream.

For example, the test subject has been made to fast, but it was not possible to prove that this made them dream more about taking food. Nor did extremely dehydrated test subjects dream particularly of drinking. So far, researchers have not dealt much with dream contents, except that some Freudians were pleased to ascertain that the Freudian formula also works with such dream material.

Since we have learned that we have several dreams every night, but on average can certainly not remember all of them, the old question of why we actually dream has become all the more pressing. Engineers interested in biology have suggested that dreaming is to be understood in computer terms as "junk removal," where it is necessary from time to time to get rid of useless information; these people regard dream elements exclusively as contents which have come into the system (also subliminally) through the sense organs and their being played back corresponds to elimination.

More serious-minded neurophysiologists think, on the contrary, that this playback has something to do with the learning process, actually with the storing of information at a molecular level (DNS), in other words with the training of the long-term memory. Be that as it may, the fact that dreaming has in itself a biological-psychological significance emerges very clearly from the large-scale tests carried out by Dement, in which the test subjects are chronically impeded from REM sleep, so-called dream deprivation (or more accurately REM deprivation). With such test subjects, nervous disturbances are said to occur, although this has not been proved beyond question. However, what is certain is that at the end of such tests the test subject has a strong need to make up for lost REM sleep, from which we can assume that there is a more or less constant need for REM and hence for dreaming.

At any rate, in addition to the physiological need for REM sleep there is a psychological need for dreaming, which thus makes the same contribution to the objectivity of dreams. We now see many test subjects who sometimes sleep in the laboratory for nights on end and in this way can artificially be made aware of all their dreams. If the Freudian censor really means well by us, makes us forget most of our dreams, and thus protects our sleep and the peace of our souls, then these test subjects, who now suddenly have to forgo this protection, should feel really alarming effects. But we were not able to ascertain any such effects.

If dreams *in themselves* have a homeostatic function, whether remembered or even analyzed or not, then dream interpreters would be mere quacks. The dreams would do their work every night like good little fairies, would get the house in order, as long as one restrained oneself and did not watch them, i.e., on no account found out how it all happened. And there are actually people who dispel their dreams just when they are out to observe them.

According to Jung's concept, the unconscious is a continuum which does not cease in the waking state but is merely drowned periodically by the noise of the conscious. But it can be seen and heard again in the periodically occurring REM phases in the dream. Thanks to the Dement-Kleitman technique we now have the possibility to glimpse behind the scenes much more frequently than under natural conditions. Thus our test subjects in the laboratory came up with 17 times as many dreams as in the earlier analytical situation. In this way we receive an amount of "information" that would normally be lost. It is reasonable to assume that this part of the information is not yet "consciousness ripe," or the other way round, that the conscious is not yet in a position to integrate it. This concept presupposes a hierarchy of the contents of the conscious in the sense of a learning or becoming conscious process which can only come about step by step.

We are quite aware of this from the waking world: we shall never be able to learn analysis without first understanding arithmetic and algebra. So under the laboratory conditions described above we shall often come up against contents that are still too far from the level of our conscious development and thus make an odd or strong impression on us, but can in no way yet be assimilated and so are forgotten again, as they are not yet capable of being remembered.

In this respect, too, the theory of the censor being the custodian of sleep would fall flat, as it does not work in any of those cases where the dream product gives us a rude awakening. On the other hand, the waking effect has the direct consequence that we remember such dreams vividly, and are thus making a connection to the conscious. Such dreams always have a strong emotional tone and for that reason alone remain in our memories, as we were able to prove in our laboratory.[72] The pronounced emotional tone of such dreams leads one to suppose that the contents must be archetypal, for clinical observation, too, confirms the connection between emotionality, archetype and memory.

Let us repeat here, in parentheses, that the empirically known connection between the occurrence of archetypal dream material and certain critical and typical phases of life urgently calls for methodically acquired evidence, as does the hierarchical succession of archetypal images in the course of life and in individual analysis. Such evidence should be obtainable using the content-analysis method of C. S. Hall and R. Van de Castle.[73]

The constant relation of archetype and emotion is one of those elementary psychological phenomena that are far from being understood. The connection with the formation of memory is clear, it is true, but is probably only a secondary effect. What is primary is an emotion (e-motio), which goes along with a large number of attendant physical symptoms (cf. Vol. I of this textbook). This reminds us that many ancient cultures were convinced of the existence of "healing dreams" (*enhypnion enarges* = effective dream), i.e., dreams that have a direct physical healing effect,[74] which can probably only be understood in this light by intuition.

The accompanying physical symptoms of complex stimuli have been dealt with in the first volume of this textbook. They can be recorded in the laboratory with highly sophisticated techniques, even during sleep. But we get the impression that on average they are nowhere near as striking and regular in their occurrence in sleep as during waking hours, so that one may have to reckon with a neurophysiological suppression. But this, too, is overcome together with the Freudian censor in the case of waking dreams or nightmares. Nevertheless, the fact remains that the periphery from which we derive these vegetative attendant symptoms is switched off more firmly in sleep than when we are awake. We retreat further into ourselves. Does that mean we reflect more about ourselves? And seen in this way, dreams perform the "internal service."

Dement thought for a long time that dreaming corresponded to a process by means of which the exhaustion substances (toxins) that accumulated in waking life could be broken down and detoxified. The theory is not really tenable for the dream (REM) phases would then have to be particularly intensive at the beginning of sleep, which is not the case. In fact the opposite applies, in that the first REM phase only occurs after a minimum of 90 minutes and the later REM periods become longer and their dream correlates correspond much better to a "drame intérieur," whereas the early REM phases promote rather short and fragmentary dreams. As the dreams of the final REM phases also contain fewer "remnants of the day," one has the impression that in the course of the night, as suggested above, we turn more toward ourselves, i.e., toward our real psychic problems and needs, and there we begin to mythologize (Synesius, cf. p. 56). Here, it seems, is where the real performance of the psyche begins, μόνος πρὸς μόνον (Plotinus) eye to eye, as it were, with the preoccupation of the day finally out of the way.

In view of the weakness of the somatic correlate that we derive from the surface, the suspicion arises that on this "structural level" (Jackson) "all comes to all," i.e., there is no longer a clear distinction between psyche and soma, that both systems in the REMP share a common, neutral language; this would mean that dream and REMP have some connection with the long-sought tertium between body and soul, and also with Jung's disconcerting principle of synchronicity.[75]

If we are abandoning the sphere of bold speculation, let us make mention of just one more theoretical informative statement on the subject: in sleep we become, to different degrees, less and less afferent, i.e., there is a massive reduction in the information gained through sensory impressions. In the tests with sensory deprivation[76] it was seen that the test subjects tended to hallucinations or fantasies, which sounds like *horror vacui*. Now in waking life, of course, we are constantly in the situation of suffering from lack of information, namely wherever we know too little, cannot see what comes next, and so on. In such situations we usually say: "it is as if . . .", whereupon a pictorial expression always follows. We would like to make a variation in Goethe's words and say: For where there are no words, an *image* appears. It may be that in sleep the soul creates these "correct images" for us in this way, in the form of dreams. If we are open to them, the gaps in our information may be filled, which would be one more interesting function of dreaming.

CHAPTER III

ANCIENT DREAM THEORIES

Nichts aber ist nötiger, als
dass man lerne eigenes Tun und
Vollbringen an das
anzuschliessen, was Andere
getan und vollbracht haben: das
Produktive mit dem Historischen
zu verbinden.
—Goethe, 1819

As we know, dreaming is a universal phenomenon, perhaps not even confined to human beings for there can be little doubt that higher mammals also dream. So the claim can be made that as far as dreaming is concerned, the psyche reveals a high degree of constancy and is rather conservative. In other words, it functions more or less in the same way at all times and in all places. We can therefore reasonably assume that the thoughts of people of other times and other cultures on dreaming have lost none of their original validity, and it would be presumptuous to dismiss them as antiquated superstitions. Of course, these ancient statements have to be translated into our language, which is no easy matter, all the more so because in the western world the psyche has practically ceased to be a term of reference in scientific discussion. This is one good reason why it needs to be "amplified," although this should not be done without considering the cultural and religious background from which the amplification material originates. *The more a widespread popular term is scientifically undermined, the more densely its un-*

44

conscious opposite number is filled, and it then plays tricks on us, as described in the first volume of this textbook.

We prefer to learn from what intelligent people have had to say about dreams, and thus not shirk the task of studying the texts from their points of view. But we need to abandon any existing prejudices *sine ira et studio*; otherwise the same thing that happened to Freud could happen to us. It is to his credit that he ploughed his way through an enormous amount of literature, and we have often referred to it. Amazingly, however, we discover that he almost completely disregards the material he so painstakingly compiled in favor of his own new theory. Fortunately, Jung did not put forward any such theory so we are not likely to fall into the same trap. We deal with the history of dream theory within the framework mentioned above.[77]

1. Egypt and the Old Testament

We know from the Old Testament that great importance was attached to dream interpretation in Ancient Egypt. This was even more the case in the Mesopotamian cultures. Our detailed knowledge about this comes from the 1956 book by A. Leo Oppenheimer,[78] who distinguishes between dream messages, symbolic dreams and mantic dreams. The most important fact is that in this culture sphere, dreams were generally understood as having been sent by the gods.

A similar attitude prevails in the Old Testament, as can be seen for example in 1. Samuel 28, 15, where the melancholic King Saul complains: "And God is departed from me, and answers me no more, neither by prophets, nor by dreams." Dream and prophecy are on a par here. Let us also refer to the thorough compilation made by Ernst Ludwig Ehrlich.[79] Hans Schär[80] has furnished evidence of the fact that with the passage of time the dream has been rejected as a means of revelation; this is particularly noticeable in the New Testament.

As for the theory of dreaming, all these sources are unproductive, not because of any shortcomings in the texts but rather because there was little or no scientific questioning of such matters. Star and dream interpretations commanded the greatest respect, but even with the stars the science of astronomy played second fiddle to astrology. Greece was the first country to develop any scientific curiosity, and we are indebted to her for so much that is worth heeding about this subject.

2. *Indian Dream Theory*

The most ancient culture for which we have detailed sources about
its theory of dreams is the Indian culture. The famous "dream key"
of Jaggaddeva was drawn up in the 12th century, although it goes
back to an age-old tradition according to which it was not possible
to tell any difference between dream and reality. Thus the reality
of tomorrow is simply a continuation of the dream, and hence must
carry out what the dream promised. The dream thus becomes
prophetic, or, as we would say, anticipatory. And in this sense the
dream is respected as a pronouncement of the divinity. Of course
it contains elements from the past but, for the reason given above,
these are trivial compared to the future. Thus we see in Indian
dream theory, as is often the case in the waking state of the Indian,
a total indifference to historical facts, and hence an utter disregard
for the Freudian remnants of the day. With the dream so tied to the
future, the dream interpreter becomes a superior figure. When this
happens with us—and it is unfortunately by no means rare—the
analyst must guard against the risk of inflation. On the other hand
we should recall Plato's δαιμόνιος ἀνήρ (*daimonios aner* = demonic
man).

In Indian theory, the dream represents the soul's experiences during its nightly excursion out of the sleeper's body; thus the dreamer
must not be wakened for it could easily happen that his soul might
not get back in time and thus he would die or go mad. We are
familiar with this concept from many primitive tribes. According
to Ramanuja,[81] however, the divinity creates a new body for the
dreamer, a dream double. Another theory dispenses with extra-
corporal experience and, on the contrary, assumes that in sleep, as
the external sensory experiences are extinguished, the inner sense,
the mana, is awake and conveys his experiences to us in the dream
(we refer here to the Aristotelian concept mentioned below). Thus
experiences from earlier existences, which form the basis of unconscious dispositions, are recapitulated, as made clear by Emil
Abegg.[82] This view is also part of Vaisheshika, the Indian natural
philosophy. Dream events from good Karma (= continuing of actions in the earlier existence) have favorable consequences, and those
from bad Karma have unfavorable ones. According to natural
philosophy, the three basic elements (*dâstu, dosha*) wind, phlegm
and gall, play a role as dream constituents and, of course, for illnesses, too. A link between Greek medicine and dream theory does
not seem unlikely in view of the passage through India of Alexander
the Great.

If there is a predominance of the windy element (= sanguine temperament), the dreamer feels he is walking through the air, hurrying across the Earth, fleeing from wild animals. If the phlegm predominates (= phlegmatic temperament), the dreamer feels he is walking across the sea, sinking in the bog, watching the downpour of rain. If the dreamer is ill-tempered (= a choleric person), he leaps into the fire, sees flashes of lightning and sees the skies burst into flames. According to this theory, dreams corresponding to the dreamer's temperament are said to be favorable omens, and those not corresponding, unfavorable ones.

The belief that the dream turns into the reality of the day gives rise to a whole series of recommended forms of behavior. We are talking here about the last dream of the night. If it is a favorable omen, it should be recounted to the Sun God on wakening. Bad dreams, on the other hand, are not talked about, for this would make them turn immediately into reality. In the latter case, one can choose to sleep on (today we would say until the next REM phase) and perhaps make the last dream a good one. A further prophylactic measure is to transport oneself before sleeping into the sphere of the God of Light, which can be brought about by meditation, bathing, asceticism, etc. Even Rigveda had special prayers to ward off bad dreams; also, "He who threads the path of virtue, is healthy, has a strong character, has control of his senses and shows pity, he will usually be sent the requested offering in his dreams." When the King has a bad dream, great lustration ceremonies are carried out, far away from residential areas (because of the risk of contamination), with up to 150 priests in attendance.

In about the year 1160, Jagaddeva[83] wrote the classical Indian dream book *Svapnacintamani* (= sleep wish jewel), after his father Denlabharaja had written the *Samudratilaka*, a handbook of the art of soothsaying. Jagaddeva stands somewhere between King David, for whom dreams came from God, and Franz Moor, for whom they came from the stomach. The tremendous number of details he gives can be explained only by the unlimited imagery world of Indian intellectual life and Pantheon. A brief introduction puts forward the casuistry of dreams of good omens, from which it emerges that as in Greece, conformity of dreams with the moral and religious circumstances has a *favorable* meaning; thus in India, as in Greece, the dream interpreter must be familiar with his mythology and folklore. Only a few examples of good dreams are given.

The list of *unfavorable* dreams, however, is much longer because it is important here to perform the correct apotropaic rites. This section of the book offers us little, although an interesting principle emerges: some dreams have a paradoxical meaning. Thus the sight of a wedding, especially one's own, is disastrous. By way of contrast, he who mourns, weeps, laments or dies in his dream experiences happiness everywhere. He who sees corpses or dies from poisoning will be healthy.[84] Enjoying intoxicating drinks, a deadly sin for the Brahmin, is a sign of luck, as is the splitting open of the head.[85] Castration means increased potency. Anyone who does repulsive things in a dream without feeling disgusted will have luck or even, in the case of mother incest, become king. When a woman dreams of being mated with a snake, she will give birth to a hero, a motif with which we are familiar from Greek mythology.[86] In general, however, apart from these exceptions, dream actions in accordance with the laws of nature are interpreted as favorable, the unnatural ones as unfavorable.

3. The Dream in Ancient Greece

In Ancient Greece the dream originally had a purely religious significance, only to fall prey later to flashy dream interpreters who came pouring in wherever there was a festival or a fair. The extraordinary variability in the meaning of the dream seems to be true not only for Greece but for many other cultures. It seems to be a sort of culture pattern, unless it is peculiar to the phenomenon of the dream as such. But the broad spectrum of significance of the dream was not only a function of the age, for conversely it can also be proved that *at the same time* the appreciation of the dream varied widely, according to the dreamer's social rank, education or philosophy. Moreover, this correlation could have been direct or the opposite, as is still the case with us today. If we wish to find a constant allowing us to bring the appreciation of the dreamer into relation with a known quantity, this is to be sought in the dreamer's attitude to be irrational. In this respect it is very significant that *one* specific phenomenon concerning the dream has survived its fluctuating market value for thousands of years, namely *incubation* (temple sleep).

Already practiced in the highly archaic caves of the god Amphiaraos in Oropos or of Trophonios in Lebadeia, incubation still flourishes in many Christian places of pilgrimage, not just in Greece (cf. Hamilton).[87] Some reasons for this striking fact are discussed later. Here is a chronological compilation of some statements made by Greek poets, philosophers and doctors about dreams.

With Homer ὄνειρος (*oneiros* = the dream) is always a personified, but divine (θεῖος, *theios*) and a winged being, who appears to
the dreamer ὑπὲρ κεφαλῆς (*hyper kephales*), i.e., at the head of the
bed and then vanishes, being independent of time and space. When,
for example, Nestor appeared to Agamemnon in a dream, he called
himself Διὸς δὲ τοι ἀγγελὸς εἰμι (*Dios de toi angelos eimi*, Iliad II. 26),
"I am a messenger of Zeus." His task is to pass on to Agamemnon
the will of God. This example may serve as a model for all Homeric
dreams, at least insofar as they all come from Zeus. In the so-called
Homeric Hermes hymn, this god is called the ἡγῆτωρ ὀνείρων (*he-
getor oneiron*), conductor and intermediary of dreams.

In Greek dreams of these early times the gods usually appear in
person and speak to the dreamer (*quod ipsi dii cum dormientibus
colloquantur*, as Cicero says in *de divin*. I. 64). As further examples let us just mention Il. X. 496 and Od. VI. 21 and XX. 32.

Passages in ancient literature clearly show that everyone was convinced that dreams were messages from the gods. Theoretically, or
rather philosophically and theologically, behind this conviction is
the Orphic equation σῶμα (*soma*) = σῆμα (*sema*) (the body is the
tomb of the soul), which we also find in Plato (Phaidros 250 C).
For in sleep the soul is released from the body, its tomb, and having thus become more sensitive, can consort with higher beings. This
idea is also found with the Pythagorians and is still alive with Aeschylos and Euripides, as well as Pindar (fr. 116 B) and Xenophon
(Cyrop. 8.7.21).

Given the fact that dreams were regarded with such reverence, it
is understandable that they were carefully observed and interpreted.
In the "Prometheus" of Aeschylos, dream interpretation is one of
Prometheus' most significant discoveries (Prom. 486). It was also
necessary to go to any lengths to ward off any evil which may have
appeared in a dream. For example, one could tell such a dream to
Helios, whose bright light would dispel the dark omens (Sophocles,
Electra 424 and Scholien, Euripides, Iphi. Taur. 42). The reader
may recall that the Indian, in accordance with his different premises,
does the exact opposite in such cases. Or one could offer sacrifices
to the apotropous gods (Xenophon, Symp. 4.33; Hippocrates, peri
enhypn. II 10 Kühn). In less drastic cases a lustration with water
seems to have sufficed (Aeschylus, Pers. 200, Aristophanes, Frogs
1339, Appollonius Rhod. IV. 662). (For further examples see Büchsenschütz.)

Another interesting aspect about dreams can be seen in Euripides
(Hecuba 70), where the Mistress of the Earth is called ὤ, πότνια

Χθῶν, μελανοπτερύγων μῆτερ ὀνείρων (*O, potnia Chthon, melanop-terygon meter oneiron*) i.e., mother of the black-winged dreams. On the strength of this chthonic (underground) origin of dreams the custom of incubation has survived into modern times.

Plato did not develop any special dream theory. All that emerges from his psychology is that the dream content depends esentially on which of the three parts of the soul is active in him, the λογιστικόν (*logistikon* = the reasonable, imaginative faculty), the θυμοειδές (*thymoeides* = the feeling, the "courage," the covetousness), or the θηριῶδές (*theriodes* = the brutal). But Plato does emphasize that when the logistikon dominates in the dream, the most profound truth can be revealed to us (Rep. IX. 571 C. ff.). As Xenophon makes clear in his commentary, such dreams have to be interpreted because they are beyond the comprehension of common knowledge. It is also known that in the Symposium (203 A) Plato calls a man who is an expert at dreams δαιμόνιος ἀνήρ (*daimonios aner* = demonic man) as opposed to the βάναυσος (*banausos* = narrow-minded man), who cannot do this. But these are the words of the Diotima, his Eros expert; according to her, demons are the originators of dreams and oracles, and one of these demons is actually Eros. Keep in mind that Plato puts these words into the mouth of a woman!

We turn briefly now to Aristotle, whose concept of the dream has had the most enduring influence. Two of his opuscula in the *parva naturalia* have come down to us in relatively good condition, allowing us an adequate look at his theory. They are 1. περὶ ἐνυπνίων (*peri enhypnion* = on the dream), and 2. περὶ τῆς καθ᾽ὕπνον μαντικῆς (*peri tes kat hypnon mantikes* = on soothsaying from dreams, especially 464b).

According to these treatises the dream is the result of the affections (p.e. 461 a 7) of the κοινὸν αἰσθετήριον (*koinon aistheterion* = common feeling), of the ἀρχὴ τῆς αἰσθήσεως (*arche tes aistheseos*), i.e., of the heart as the central seat of ideas, caused by the minimal movements which remain from the activity of the sense organs in the waking state. For this common feeling French psychiatry has kept the term *cénesthésie*. This is the *sensus communis*, also known as common sensibility or common sensation. Other authors talk of organ or vitality sensibility. Herbart uses the expression *Gesam-tempfindung* (total sensibility) or *Totalgefühl* (total feeling). There are also occasional references to somatic consciousness. The term is anything but clear. Often it can be well-being, desire, reluctance, or weariness. The clearest term is the French *troubles cénesthé-*

siques, as they occur when there is a dangerous assault on the unconscious, for example in the initial stages of a spell of schizophrenia. They are also very accurately depicted by Lewis Carroll at the beginning of *Alice's Adventures in Wonderland.*

Aristotle speaks of a κοινὴ δύναμις ἀκολουθοῦσα πάσαι (*koine dynamis akolouthousa pasai*), i.e., a *dynamis* common to all sensory qualities. Of course, these movements are also there in the waking state, but are not perceived, not heard, since the sensory organs are moving violently. Because of the violent actions from outside they make far too great a noise to allow for any additional self-perception. We are reminded of Lorenzo's statement in Shakespeare's *Merchant of Venice* (V/1): "Such harmony is in immortal Souls; / But whilst this muddy venture of decay / Doth grossly close it in, we cannot hear it."

Thus prophetic dreams are possible, for in sleep the dreamer is much more sensitive to slight disturbances of an organic nature, so that an experienced doctor can use dreams to forecast an illness or its cure, as well as death.

According to Aristotle, dreams about people we know well can also be prophetic. This can be explained simply by the fact that we also know their motivations, and our consciousness becomes involved with these people and their problems, so that from this knowledge we can draw certain conclusions about how these people will act in the future. This concept, *nota bene*, claims to be a strictly rational one!

A further similar aspect of dreams, according to Aristotle, is that they can prompt the dreamer to specific actions in the future. Concerning the diagnostic and prognostic use of dreams, Aristotle closes his treatise on "Prophecies from Dreams" with an interesting comparison on how dreams can and should be understood and interpreted:

> The best dream interpreter is the one who has the ability to recognize similarities. With "similarity" I mean the following: images of the imagination are like reflection images in the water, as I mentioned earlier. In the latter case when there is movement the reflection is not like the original, nor are the images like the real object. So a talented interpreter of such reflections would be the one who can quickly make the distinction and recognize that the broken and distorted fragments of the image represent a person or, for example, a horse or any other object. In the first case, too, the dream has a somewhat similar result, for the movement disturbs the clarity of the dream image.

Paradoxically one could say, if one were generalizing, that Aristotle is of the same opinion as Diotima in that he traces dreams back to *demonic* origins. He argues *per exclusionem* that they could not come from God as they would then only be sent to the best and wisest people, which obviously is not the case. This conclusion contains a general devaluation of the dream, which had a long-lasting negative influence on its reputation in the Western world.

It is clear that the Epicureans as well as the new Academy (Carneades) had just as little time for dreams as the Cynics. But in the Stoa, dreams once again become fashionable. The school head Zenon, for example, is reported to have said that the students could read from their own dreams how much progress they had made in virtue. The old Stoa seems to have drawn up the first classification of dreams, and done so according to their origins (St. V.F. 3.605): Either they come from God or from the demons, or else they are the product of the activity of the soul itself. Moreover, the Stoics regard prophecy through dreams as possible, on the basis of the connection between the human soul and the world soul. On the basis of this relation, man perceives the link between all things, when his senses are at rest, i.e., in sleep, and in this way he is capable of knowing the future (St. V.F. 2.1198). Poseidonios (Cic.*de div.* 1.30) explains that there are three ways that the divine can influence Man in dreams:

1. The soul can see the future thanks to its own divine nature.
2. The air is full of immortal souls which bear manifest signs of the truth and are able to penetrate into the sleeper's system through the pores (πόροι) of the sensory organs (Plutarch, de plac. phil. V. 2 und quaest. conviv. VIII. 10, 2).
3. The gods themselves speak to the sleepers (cf. Reinhardt, Poseid. 457/9).

Incidentally, in Plutarch (Fragm. 178) we come across a concept which is a striking reminder of the speculation (see above) which we ventured on concerning the function of REM sleep.

χωρίζεται γὰρ [ἡ ψυχὴ] ἐν τῷ καθεθίδειν
ἀνατρέχουςα καὶ συλλεγομένη, πρὸς ἑαυτὴν
ἐκ τοῦ διατετάσθαι πρὸς τὸ σῶμα καὶ
διεσπάρθαι ταῖς αἰσθήσεσι

Plutarch, Moralia, Fragm. 178, peri psyches; Translation:

For in sleep the soul is dissociated in that it retreats and concentrates on itself (gathers itself, collects itself), after being extended before, so as to give life to the body, and having been diffused by the sensory organs.

This concept, together with the famous correspondence of macro- and microcosmos, seem to provide a causal explanation for all mantic beliefs: the order of the universe consists of the linkings of *causa* with *effectus*; certain signs enable us to recognize certain *causae*, which are bound to lead to certain *effectus*. These signs, for their part, are perceived in certain dreams (Cic. *de div*: *Poseidonius esse censet in natura signa quadam rerum futurarum*).

Although this theory makes possible those dreams that are precognitive or prophetic, or rather those dreams which have to be understood in this sense, we have to turn to another theory for telepathic dreams, and amazingly enough we find it in Democritus. His atoms are, as we know, εἴδωλα (*eidola*), images, and all have characteristics of the *Individuum*, a Latin word that had to be recoined by Cicero when he wanted to translate the Democritic ἡ ἄτομος (*he atomos* = the atom) for his fellow Romans. Insofar as the air is full of atoms = individuals, these atoms are naturally suitable bearers of messages from one person to another, which in theory makes it easy for telepathic effects to come about (Cic. *de div*. I.43 and II.67). As I have already produced one anachronism by referring back to Democritus, let me produce one more on this subject by recalling the famous fr. 89D of Heraclitus: τοῖς ἐγρηγορόσιν ἕνα καὶ κοινὸν κόσμον εἶναι, τῶν δὲ κοιμωμένων ἕκαστον εἰς ἴδιον ἀποστρέφεσθαι: "those who are awake have one and one common world, but in sleep each turns away from it and to his own." *His own* must be his dream world, and he is there for himself alone and with himself alone, in a sort of primal situation. This is per se a mythological situation and consequently dream events are actually of a *cosmogonic* nature, which is what Jung means when he recommends understanding dreams on the "subjective level" as well.

We now outline briefly the attitude of Greek *medicine* toward dreams. To do this we must go back to the fifth century where we find a special tract on dreams in Pseudo-Hippocrates (περὶ ἐνυπνίων, *peri enhypnion*, T. II 1–16 Kühn). He asserts that in the waking state the soul is preoccupied with bodily functions, whereas in sleep it is the unrestricted lord of the manor, for the sleeping body has no powers of perception. Consequently, when the body is asleep, the soul, which is ever awake, has all the physiological and psychological functions at its own disposal. Thus a doctor who knows how to assess this correlation correctly possesses a considerable amount of wisdom. Furthermore, Hippocrates also admits that divine influence can manifest itself in dreams and so we can learn things from them that we would otherwise never know. As far as the diagnostic value of dreams is concerned, he believes that in sleep the dream can pick up the causes of illness in *images*. Here for the first time we can see that it is assumed that the psyche has a symbolic function. As for the medical aspect of the dream, Hippocrates shows very clearly that the health of the dreamer is reflected in the dream. With him there are, however, dreams that are purely divine in inspiration, and the exegesis of such dreams he leaves to the specialized dream interpreter.

Then there are also the *natural* influences through which the soul perceives the state of the body and in this way becomes a "hygienic system" which functions as follows: as long as the dream simply repeats what went on during the day (one thinks automatically of Freud's "remnants of the day"), the body is apparently in order. But when the dream is about conflict, war and such matters, this means that things are not well with the body. Thus, for example, it is a sign of good health if we dream about the sun and moon as they are in nature. But when they appear in our dreams and something is wrong with them, then there must be something wrong with those systems of our body which, in accordance with the equation macrocosmos = microcosmos, correspond to these "planets." We are reminded at this point of what we referred to earlier as the medieval correspondences between planets, zodiac and human body, as they were used in medicine in the Melotheses (bloodletting man) (cf. fig. 5 p. 34). Springs and fountains correspond to the uropoietic system, rivers to the circulation system, so that for example, floods or droughts respectively correspond diagnostically to hypertension or anemia (cf. the "hippocratic" book περὶ διαίτης, *peri diaites*, IV. 88ff.).

Galen had little more or different to say about the problem. As can be seen clearly from the example just quoted, the diagnosis is made from the dream text with the aid of a technique which can certainly be aptly described as "analogy thinking." This technique was described by several ancient authorities as the only important point in the art of dream interpretation (Arist. *div.p.somn.* (s.o.) 464 b5; Artemid. II.25).

In fact there is not really anything essentially new in the dream theories of Hippocrates and Galen, compared to Plato, Aristotle and Democritus, for even Plato and Aristotle had the idea that dreams derive from the perception of the reverberating movements left over from the waking life (τὰς ἐντὸς κινήσεις, *tas entos kineseis* with Plato or κινήσεις φανταστικαὶ ἐν τοῖς αἰσθητερίοις, *kineseis phantastikai en tois aistheteriois* with Aristotle). The psychology of Aristotle could be termed a differential calculus of the reciprocal inhibitions, stimulations, super-positions and interferences of these internal movements. For purely medicinal purposes there had to be a forgoing of any acceptance of "external" dream sources, and also of the *"somnia a deo missa"* of Macrobius. Here we come up against a fundamental difference regarding the concept of a transcendental or an immanent source of dreams; this difference arose through the rationalistic medical orientation which, since Hippocrates, has almost completely done away with the original purely religious attitude toward dreams. Yet the divination from dreams of hidden physical conditions has never stopped. (I produced two examples of this kind in my inaugural lecture at the E.T.H.[88] The Halle Professor of Rhetoric Friedrich August Wolf (1759–1824) made the following comment on this subject: "Perhaps when nobody believes any longer in animal magnetism, one will learn oneself to arouse the divination spirit in sick people by new and more certain methods."[89]

The Greeks were almost exclusively interested in a transcendental source. Dreams were regarded as objective facts, as something that actually happened to one. The Greek was "visited" by a dream (ἐπισκοπεῖν, *episkopein*), or he also said he had "seen" a dream (ἐνύπνιον ἰδεῖν, *enhypnion idein*). It would never have occurred to him to say *"J'ai fait un rêve"* or *"Ho fatto un sogno."* But then came the rationalistic epoch described above, and this in turn was replaced by the swing of the pendulum. In the Hellenistic era, for example, Philon was known to regard the πνεῦμα (*pneuma*) as the most important organ. It was ψυχὴ ψυχῆς (*psyche psyches*), the soul of the soul, and had the purest and best οὐσία (*ousia*), real nature, namely, a divine one. For Philon the dream was a phenomenon that played a major role in the spirit. Hence all dreams were important because of their prophetic quality. He saw three categories of dreams: (1) prophetic dreams through direct divine influence, (2) dreams that are prophetic through the exercise of reason insofar as this is "in harmony" with the general divine rhythm, and (3) prophetic dreams which derive from *purely psychic* emotions, on the basis of divinely inspired forces. Only the dreams in this last category need interpreting, although of course their element of divine inspiration betrays their divine origins, so that once again, as we can see, *everything becomes irrational.*

Of course, this one-sided divinely inspired concept is just as inadequate as the purely rationalistic one. The early distinction made by Homer (Od. XIX. 560ff.) should never be forgotten: There will always be confused, relatively unimportant dreams which make their way through the ivory gates, and also clear and very significant dreams that come through the gates of horn. (I should like to point out about this famous passage that Penelope's dream about the geese and the eagle is interpreted purely allegorically and in no way symbolically in the Jungian sense.) It is precisely this dichotomy which makes it possible to take dreams seriously, as was most impressively the case with those Greek dreamers who presented sacrifices and had temples built because of their dreams (Aristides).

I am inclined to accept the fact that almost all the observations made by the Greeks about dreams are still valid. Of course, because of cultural changes some things are no longer found. With us, for example, everything has become so secularized that there are hardly any more divine epiphanies in our dreams. For the same reason, it is no longer true that only kings, priests or doctors have big dreams.

The material presented so far had to be compiled carefully and painstakingly, from widely scattered sources. Büchsenschütz took it upon himself to do this, as did Dodds later, albeit from one special approach. Sad to say, all the important books on dreams, of which there were a fair number in ancient times, have been lost. This means we have to depend on authors of the second and fourth centuries A.D., who have at least handed down summaries of the original works. The most important experts are Artemidorus of Daldis (known as Daldianus although he was actually born in the Ephesus of the mystery cult), Macrobius and Synesius of Cyrene. Artemidorus had the advantage of knowing all the ancient literature on dreams and because he spent his life as a professional dream interpreter, had the benefit of wide practical experience. He carefully collected and evaluated over 3000 dreams, and had a good look at the dreamers and their past histories as well; moreover, he followed each case to find out the real outcome of each dream. There is no disputing the fact that his interest was a scientific one, which I should like to stress because he is not taken seriously enough. The reasons for people's prejudices against him would be well worth a careful psychological analysis.

Macrobius and Synesius were much more educated men in comparison, who thought about dreams more independently and bothered less about the literature on the subject. But they were *philosophical scholars* and did not actually practice. Thus Macrobius was initiated into the mysteries of neoplatonism and Synesius was made a Christian bishop, although he still had not been baptized and had a wife and children, which is an indication of how highly he was respected for his culture and education. This is why it was essential that he should at all costs be won over to Christianity; he became bishop only with reluctance, on condition that he might be allowed to "philosophize at home and mythologize in church" (ψιλοσοφῶν and φιλομνθῶν, *philosophon* and *philomython*). Whereas it can be said of Artemidorus that he was an eclectic, Macrobius and Synesius strongly adhered to their neoplatonist school; Synesius is said to have been the first neoplatonist to be baptized.

(a) Macrobius

At the end of de re publica (VI. 1-9), Cicero gives what is reputed to be the dream of Scipio Africanus Minor, which represents a genuine great myth. In this he is following his great model Plato, who also liked to end his dialogues with a myth.[90]

In this case the prototype is the "Politeia," which concludes with the myth of ER. The text of the Somnium Scipionis is available today in an edition of the "Philosophische Bibliothek" Meiner.[91] Macrobius wrote a detailed commentary in two volumes about this report by Cicero: "*Commentariorum ex Cicerone in Somnium Scipionis libri duo.*" This book became very popular and once the art of printing was perfected was reissued several times. There are modern translations in the "Collection des Auteurs Latins"[92] and an English one by William Harris Stahl.[93] Macrobius owes his fame to the seven books "Saturnalia," dialogues in which an immense number of philological, historical and mythological questions are treated. He lived about 400 A.D. and in 410 was pro-consul in Africa. The effects of his writings on Scipio's dream were significant. M. Schedler[94] carefully traced these effects, which covered science and theology, up to the late Middle Ages. The work of Macrobius also influenced the world of music, for the popular story inspired the young Mozart (1771) to compose an "azione musicale" entitled "Il sogno di Scipione" (K.V.126), based on the text of Metastasio. As regards the purely philological aspect, we shall simply mention H. Linke.[95]

Here is some background history of the dream: Scipio Africanus Minor (185-129 B.C.) was the conqueror of Carthage and Numantia. According to Cicero he achieved the compromise between Greek and Roman intellectual life and was friendly with Polybius and Panaitius. He was made consul before being of legal age for the position. He was murdered in the year 129. He had the dream under discussion while he was a soldier in Africa because he was "initiated into philosophy" as it says, having spoken the previous evening with Massinissa (King of Numidia) and Scipio Africanus Major, his grandfather.

Summarized briefly, the dream runs as follows:

Scipio Africanus Major appears to him and foretells that in two years
he will destroy Carthage. At first he will be sent to different countries as a legate, then he will become consul, then dictator and
restorer of the State. He will attain the highest honors unless he is
murdered by relatives. Then comes a long exposition on the soul,
basically a comprehensive representation of contemporary psychology. When it says that those who are outstanding for "virtutes" will
live on after death, Scipio wants to kill himself at once. Stop! it says.
Only the gods can take you away. To help him to understand, he is
given a visual instruction, just like with Virgil and later with Dante:
the sky with its nine spheres, where he hears the sphere of music, he
is shown the earth with its zonal divisions, and finally the immortal-
ity and divinity of the soul is revealed to him. *Deum te igitur scito
esse!* Know then that you are divine.

Macrobius then comes in with his neoplatonist commentary,
which at times was held to be a Timaeus commentary. His sources
are Porphyry and Plotinus, and there are also a number of Virgil
quotations. The πρῶτον ἅτιον (*proton aition* = original cause) is
God and from him come the nous and the psyche. The latter passes
through a descensus through the spheres, where it takes on the
different characteristics of the planets, as with Plato earlier: from
Saturn comes reason and logic, from Jupiter energy, from Mars
ardor, from the sun feeling and fantasy, from Venus wishes and
desire, from Mercury expressiveness and from the moon generative
power, the *natura plantandi et augendi corpora*, a hyleatic-sublunar
quality. On its journey it crosses the ecliptic as it goes down into
Cancer and in the resurrection after death into Capricorn; Cancer
and Capricorn are the two *portae solis* (as with Porphyry in De antro
Nymphar. 28).

Originally the soul is a monadic sphere, but in its descent becomes
a dyad as it falls into the hyle. From this it becomes intoxicated and
descends further on the Milky Way (Plato, Phaedrus).

From the seventeenth century there is a striking parallel to the
spherical form of the prenatal, monadic soul of Plato, and this has
come down to us from Vinzenz von Paul (1567–1622, Paris).[96] He
tells of St. Francis of Sales (1567–1622, Paris).[96] He tells of St. Francis of Sales (1567–1622, Geneva), a church teacher and Bishop of
Geneva ("Monseigneur" in the text), who, with his friend Johanna
Franziska von Chantal (1572–1641, Geneva) founded the order of
the Salesians (La Visitation). The passage reads as follows:

When Mrs. de Chantal died, nineteen years after the Monseigneur, nearly a quarter of a century would pass before his canonization. She used those nineteen years to spread his fame, publish his works, and establish his order. This Visitation was comprised of eighty-six convents at the time that she passed away, quietly, while visiting the convent in Moulins. While in Paris, the director, Mr. Vincent, upon hearing of her illness, had begun to pray for her. Then he had a vision which, humbly, without speaking of himself, he related in the following words to the young women of the Visitation: ". . . A person worthy of our trust, one who would rather die than tell a lie, told me that . . . a small sphere, as if made of fire, appeared to him, rose from the earth, and united in the upper level of the air with another sphere, larger and more luminous, and that the two, now one, rose still higher and were engulfed by another sphere, infinitely larger and more glowing than the others. He was told by a voice within that this small sphere was the soul of our worthy mother, the second that of our blessed Father, and the third, the divine essence. He was left with the inner feeling that her (Mrs. de Chantal's) soul was in a state of holiness and had no need of his prayers."

What could make one doubt this vision, is that this person was convinced of the sanctity of her soul, but what makes one think that it is a real vision is that he did not usually have visions and that this was the only one he had had.[97]

In Cicero's text Scipio Africanus Major says to his grandson:

For when your age reaches 8×7 recurring revolutions of the sun, and when these two numbers, each of which is a full one, but for different reasons, have completed the number of years granted to you, in accordance with the natural rotation, then the eyes of the whole fatherland will be turned towards you and your name . . . provided you escape the hands of your kinsmen (Chap. 5).

This passage provides Macrobius with the opportunity to go into the numbers speculation which was so popular in his day. We confine ourselves here to a few details of interest psychologically although we return later to the "mathematics of the unconscious."

Initially, it is a conditional prophecy of life span: $7 \times 8 = 56$ years. In actual fact, the dreamer was killed at that age, for he did not escape the "iniquitous hands" of his kinsmen. Macrobius now speculates in pythagorian style on number symbolism: the body is changeable and transitory, whereas numbers are eternal values (*tetraktys* = four, *dekas* = ten, etc.). The 7 corresponds to the number of the planets, the 8 is twice four (*tetraktys*) or $4 + 4$ or $2 + 2 + 2 + 2$ (dyad); it is made up of the prime number 7, to which the monad 1 is added. It is therefore very important and counts as "full" (plenus); 7 is also the number of the ancient "organs." The prophecy remains ambiguous; a dream just shows *possibilities*. At best man can take heed of warnings and act accordingly.

Macrobius goes on to give a *systematics of dreams*. He separates them into five classes, under the influence of ancient colleagues (hence the Greek terms):

1. ὄνειρος
   (*oneiros*)   = *somnium*   = Big dream
2. ὅραμα
   (*horama*)   = *visio*   = Look into the future
3. χρηματισμός
   (*chrematismos*)   = *oraculum*   = A venerable person appears and tells us what we have to do.
4. ἐνύπνιον
   (*enhypnion*)   = *insomnium* = Everyday events that are unimportant. Love, food, money, enemies, reputation. These are essentially remnants of the day. The insominium can come from three sources:
     a) mental distress
     b) physical distress (physical irritations)
     c) worries about the future.
5. φάντασμα
   (*phantasma*)   = *visum*   = Hypnagogic and hypnopompic visions in the half-sleeping stage. They derive from excessive passion.

Classes 4 and 5 are dismissed as being unimportant. On the other hand, 1 is split into five subdivisions:
(a) *s. proprium*: deals with the dreamer himself.
(b) *s. alienum*: deals with other people.
(c) *s. commune*: a group of people experiences shared dream activity.
(d) *s. publicum*: deals with the community (agora, theatre).

(e) *s. generale*: the Universe speaks to the dreamer to tell him something new.

Now according to Macrobius, Scipio's dream corresponds to the three main categories 1 to 3, for it is

1. A big dream, because it cannot be understood without interpretation.

2. A *visio*, because the dreamer sees the place after his death.

3. An *oraculum*, because father (Paullus) and grandfather speak to him as venerable people.

Furthermore, it also corresponds to the five subcategories of the *somnium*. It is a

(a) *s. proprium*, in that *he*, the dreamer, is led into higher regions.

(b) *s. alienum*, in that he sees other souls in the kingdom of the dead.

(c) *s. commune*, in that with them he experiences something that wili also belong to him after death.

(d) *s. publicum*, in that there is talk of victory over Carthage.

(e) *s. generale*, in that it perceives the celestial movements and music of the spheres.

Thus we are given, together with many other details which I cannot include here, a thorough presentation of the psychology of the time, which explains why Macrobius was a significant influence for centuries. At the end the author makes it clear that Scipio's dream is nothing less than an initiation into the mysteries of the soul, culminating, as we have already said, in its becoming divine.

(b) Synesius

The tract περὶ ἐνυπνίων (*peri enhypnion*[98] = about the dream) by Synesius is not a dream book like that of Artemidorus. Such books are rejected by him on the grounds that they can only offer general explanations, without doing justice to the individuality of each soul. In contrast to such literature, but also to a certain extent in contrast to the reasoning above, he launches into an exclusively theoretical discussion of the subject. But his philosophical premises are also neoplatonic and so the tract, like that of Macrobius, was often regarded as a Timaeus commentary. Synesius' sources have been investigated by Volkmann,[99] Geffcken[100] and W. Lang;[101] they all agree in tending toward Plotinus and Porphyry. But there are also stoic elements, and Sextus Empiricus, and, especially when it comes to the doctrine of mutual sympathy, Posidonius.

Synesius was born about 370–75 A.D. and lived in Cyrene. He claims Heracles as ancestor. His teacher in Alexandria was Hypatia.

The tract under discussion must have been written when he was still a heathen, more precisely, about 404 A.D., at divine command, as he says. It was written in one night, and two or three times Synesius felt like somebody else, as if he were listening to himself. The work gave rise to animated discussion and although strongly criticized by Nikephoros Gregoras, enjoyed high esteem,[102] at least up to the Renaissance, when it was admired by Marsilio Ficino and was reprinted several times (Venice 1516 and 1518, Lyon 1549, Paris 1586 and 1612). Synesius was baptized and made bishop in the year 410.[103]

Here is a description of his concept:

As dreams were used exclusively for the purpose of divination, their theory is based on the *sympatheia* of the cosmos, which is the philosophical essence of his discourse. The second theoretical premise for dream divination is his doctrine of the fantasy.

In the introduction, Synesius says: "If dreams have prophetic powers, and dream history gives people puzzling hints about things they will really experience, then we must accord them the rating of scholarship, not, admittedly, that of clarity, unless the unclear is actually regarded as the scholarly." "The art of soothsaying is probably the supreme good" (131 A). Regarding the sympathy doctrine, Synesius argues as follows: "If divination announces everything through everything in advance, as everything is related that belongs to a living being, in our case the cosmos, and if all this behaves to a certain extent like different letter characters—Phoenician, Egyptian or Assyrian, as we find them in books, then the wise man must also be able to read it" (132 A).

This reading is possible on the basis of the following equations (134 A): the nous is to the soul as the being is to the becoming. In other words, the soul has within it the images of the becoming, which is why latent in everyone's soul is the ability to look into the future. In these images we recognize the Platonic *eidola*. These images are reflected in the *fantasy*. The nous, however, only makes itself felt in the soul as its mediating organ, thanks precisely to the *fantasy*. True, the soul contains all the *forms* of becoming (with Jung we would say: archetypes), but most of them are latent in time. Only those that are beneficial are allowed to appear to be conscious.

But the mirror in which the images, which have their seat in the soul, reveal themselves is called *fantasy*, as A. Ludwig[104] aptly remarks. So this is the organ that raises the contents of man's soul to a conscious level. Only then do we *recognize* when the "imprints" of the soul are reflected by the fantasy. It is a "life in a somewhat lower form and exists in its own natural right" (134 B). As a living being it also has sensory organs, which may be of greater value than the purely physical ones.

It is the "imaginative pneuma," the most comprehensive sensory organ, the sense of all the senses (135 D), the σῶμα πρῶτον ψυχῆς (*soma proton psyches*) and is also highly individual. So it has organs of perception: "We see colors, hear noises (in dreams) and have the clearest notion of feeling without the (corresponding) physical organs being active, and who knows whether or not this type of perception must command greater respect." It sees, it hears, in short feels things *inwardly*, thereby bringing about the soul's intercourse with the divine. "It sees with the whole pneuma, and hears with the whole pneuma" (136 A). Whereas the fantasy has here an intermediate position between soul and body, the pneuma has a very similar position like in the Corpus Hermeticum; in this context reference must be made to the works of Reitzenstein[105] and Leisegang.[106] The pneuma is the soul's first and real vehicle (ὄχημα, *ochema*)[107] "it is borderland between the rational and the irrational, the physical and the non-physical, and common ground for both, and through its offices the divine comes into contact with matter" (137 A).

Synesius continues: "The one, it says, will be taught while awake, the other while asleep. But with the one who is awake it is a person who does the teaching, and with the sleeping one it is a god" (135 B). In this connection there then follows a remarkable sentence: "For allowing something to be enjoyed is more than just teaching" (135 B). This probably refers to the immediate effect of the dream. The experiencing quality of the dream is very much in the foreground.

> The dream's here still. Even when I wake it is
> Without me, as within me; not imagin'd, felt.
> —Shakespeare, *Cymbeline*
> Act IV. Sc.ii 306–7

Shakespeare's words show us that one of the many facets of his universality was the fact that he, too, was fully aware of the immediate effect of the dream.

Then Synesius becomes more personal in an apologia for divination: "Divination must not be neglected for it paves the way to God" (143 A). "So it is my wish that this kind of soothsaying be bestowed upon me and that I can bequeath it to my children as a legacy. To gain possession of it, it is not necessary to cover a long

distance with heavy baggage, or to travel to a foreign land such as
Delphi or the shrine of Ammon; it is enough to go to sleep having
washed one's hands and said one's prayers" (143 D). In this sense
the dream is democratic and benevolent in that it is accessible to all
(unlike with Aristotle). Thus each person is his own instrument in
dream divination (145 C). "Thus man and woman should concern
themselves with dream divination, old and young, poor and rich,
ruler and subject, etc.," for it is "a good and discreet adviser" (146
A); in the promise given in the dream we have a pledge from God
and thus we can either look forward to events in advance or prepare
ourselves properly to meet them (146 D). Dreams are reconnoiterers,
patrols into the future.[108]

Synesius explains that he himself owes a lot to dream divination
and gives a few examples (148 B, D).

The best method of learning dream divination is, of course, a
good philosophical education, approaching affects with tranquillity
and a sober, frugal and sensible way of living (150 A, B). Aristotle had had the right approach when he said that perception led to
recollection, recollection to experience, experience to scientific
methods, which is equally true of dream interpretation. But once
again he emphasizes that unfortunately the pneumatic nature of
dreams does not allow for a universally valid theory and that what
is not clear becomes even less clear if torn apart (152 C). "Thus one
should forget the idea of universally valid laws; each person must
make himself the substratum of his art and should inscribe in his
memory what events happen to him and on the basis of which dream
history" (152 C).

At the end Synesius calls on the reader to note down his dreams,
and in addition to his diaries, to keep so-called night journals as the
real documents of his own way of life.[109]

Another interesting statement (154 D) is "myths owe to dreams
the ease with which they have been passed on," or, as we would say
in Jungian terms, they are made of the same material.

(c) Artemidorus

Artemidorus (second half of the second century A.D.) is dealt
with here at somewhat greater length. His work, called "*Oneirocritica*," consists of five books, and he claims to have written it at
Apollo's command. In it we find much that we proudly regard as
achievements of modern times. Attention is drawn here to only certain points, but they are based on the critical examination of 3000
dreams. And for each of these cases, Artemidorus has an anamnesis, a catamnesis and an epicrisis.

1. Probably the most striking contrast between Artemidorus' dream material and contemporary examples lies in the fact that with him epiphanies of gods are frequent occurrences. For these cases, he has a quite specific and absolutely reliable criterion, namely

2. if the god appears with all the attributes appropriate to his cult image, his appearance is interpreted as a good omen. But if there is anything even slightly "wrong" about his "accoutrements," the dream is a fateful one.[110] If gods appear in the wrong dress, what they have to say is probably deceitful. Such deviations from the norm in the divine sphere seem to have been regarded as blasphemous. The correct psychological interpretation was that such a dreamer must be in conflict with that inner truth or quality for which the corresponding god stood. Accordingly, the god had to take his revenge on the dreamer. Here, generally speaking, we come across certain common denominators of all ancient dream interpretation, and they are as follows:

3. that dreams are mainly understood as referring to future events and that they indicate

4. whether the event will be favorable or unfavorable.

5. The god, too, has to abide by certain rules, for example goddesses are more fitting for women than for men. Here, too, it is a case of "*suum cuique*" (to each his own).

6. The gods can confine themselves to appearing just in the form of their attributes (*pars pro toto*). The dream interpreter had to be well versed in mythology, as can be seen in 2 above.

7. The gods can make certain stipulations, and indeed in the event of illness can even write prescriptions. But these are always very simple and need no interpreting. The gods always speak a clear language in dreams. If they are puzzling, the sole purpose is to make us think more about the dream (IV. 22).

8. There are two kinds of dreams: a) θεωρηματικοί (*theorematikoi*), b) ἀλληγορικοί (*allegorikoi*). The former correspond exactly to reality and will soon *tale quale* come true. The latter have a deeper meaning which expresses itself δἰ αἰνιγμάτα (through *aenigmata*), and it takes a long time, maybe years, for them to come true.

9. There are dreams that come from within and those that come from outside. Any dream which contains unexpected elements belongs to the latter, for they have been sent by the gods (θεόπεμπτον, *theopempton*).

Attention should now be drawn to certain details regarding principles of interpretation which seem to me still relevant today:

1. There are only a few standard interpretations of typical dream elements; the following list is more or less complete:

Head = father

Business = mother, for it provides food.

Business = wife, because the husband is as involved with his business as with her.

Foot = slave

Right hand = father, son, friend, brother.

Left hand = wife, mother, mistress, daughter, sister.

Pudendum = parents, wife, children.

2. All dreams contain the following six elements (στοιχεία, *stoicheia*): (a) nature, (b) law, (c) custom, (d) professional skill, (e) art, and (f) name. Everything in the dream that proceeds in accordance with its nature, its law, etc., is a good omen, but anything that deviates in any way is a bad one.

3. One has to be very familiar with the dreamer's life history (anamnesis) and his current situation and in certain circumstances acquire indirect information about him (obj. anamnesis).

4. One also has to know the dreamer's character.

5. Even his mood of the moment has to be taken into consideration.

6. One has to have the complete dream text. Fragments should not be interpreted (I. 12).

7. One has to be familiar with the local customs and habits of the dreamer's milieu, so that, bearing in mind point 2, the dream can be correctly interpreted.

8. The etymology of a word should always be taken into account, especially with proper names (e.g. Eutychos = Felix = the happy one).

9. Dream motifs are ambivalent. Here are some examples:

    (a) To have donkey's ears is only a good omen for philosophers, for the donkey doesn't listen and doesn't give way. For all other dreamers it means servitude and misery (I. 24).

    (b) To take a bath: people used to do that after hard work, so it meant sweat and tears, but today it is a sign of wealth and luxury, i.e., a good omen (I. 64).

    (c) Sleeping in the temple means recovery for the sick, but illness for the healthy (I. 79).

    (d) Gold is actually a good omen, but if, for example, a man is wearing a gold neckband, it means the opposite (II. 5).

    (e) To be struck by lightning means losing everything one has. As the poor man possesses poverty, and the rich man wealth, such a dream can be a good or a bad omen (II. 9).

(f) A dolphin *in* the water is a good omen, *not in* the water a bad one (II. 16).

(g) If something bad happens to your enemies, it is a good omen for you (I. 2).

(h) If you are happy, and you are promised happiness in a dream, that means unhappiness; if you are unhappy, happiness. Conversely, if you are unhappy and dream that you will be unhappy, that means happiness.

(i) Simple people dream in concrete and direct terms, whereas for those who know a lot about dreams the bare facts in dreams are translated, as it were, into symbols (IV. intro.). One can recognize the Sophocles tradition here: "For wise men he is the creator of dark pronouncements; For stupid men he is a bad teacher but a clear one." (Nauck, Fragm. Soph. 704).

(j) The general rule is that we have pleasant dreams when we live under bad conditions. In explaining this ambivalence or multivalence of the dream symbols, Artemidorus simply points out that the facts of life itself are also ambivalent.

(k) IV. 67 gives a very impressive example of seven different interpretations of the same dream, which was dreamt by seven different pregnant women: they had all dreamt they had given birth to a snake. The interpretation had to be adapted to the personal circumstances of each of the women for, as it transpired, the outcomes (ἀπόβασις, *apobasis*) were all different too.

(l) The fulfillment of wishes in dreams is provided for by Artemidorus in the sense that he says: We want God to help us to recognize more clearly what is going on inside us. In this sense we are αἰτηματικοί, *aitematikoi*, i.e., we are inclined to ask what our dreams are, too. But he warns us clearly not to ask the gods for something that is not right and proper. Nor should we forget to offer a sacrifice and to express our thanks once our requests have been graciously answered (IV. 2).

(m) As for dream interpretation, all these and many other rules must be combined, and the possible effect on the dreamer's personality must also be borne in mind before we make our pronouncement (III. 66). Some dreams must remain uninterpreted (ἄκριτος, *akritos*) even *before* they come true (ἀπόβασις) (IV. 24).

(n) In IV. 20 Artemidorus gives a piece of advice that I would like to quote for the benefit of certain overly-scholarly analysts: after conscientious consideration of all the circumstances mentioned, one should give the interpretation simply and clearly and not try to lend it greater credibility by referring to several such and such authorities, for that would be simply trying to impress the client with one's scholarliness and intelligence. This remark and many others on the professional ethics of the dream interpreter are often apt and quite modern.

As they are characteristic of the mentality of the whole period, let us look at a few odd details which have only added to the opinion that Artemidorus is an obscurant.

(IV. 24): Alexander the Great had unsuccessfully laid siege to the city of Tyros in Phoenicia for seven months. Then one night he had a dream in which a satyr (Σάτυρος, *satyros*) appeared; the following day the city fell. Artemidorus' interpretation is: Σάτυρος was to be split up into σὰ τύρος, *sa tyros* = Tyros is yours! Of course this happened after the event, but the idea is just to illustrate the method which was often used for "prophetic" interpretations, too. In this context, let us recall that dreams really do go in for plays on words, and that in waking life, too, plays on words often get to the heart of a problem. The fact that the unconscious can be rather amusing often provides a diversion for both doctor and patient alike.

The use of the so-called "isopsephisms" in ancient dream interpretation goes much further in this direction. In Greek, as in other languages, there are no numerical figures; they are expressed by letters of the alphabet. By adding them together, each word acquires a specific numerical value. Words with the same numerical value are regarded as synonymous, and this is what the speculation of isopsephes (ἰσόψηφα) consists of. Isopsephes can be interchanged at will (as with Satyros—*sa Tyros*), which is an important factor in proficient dream interpreting. Artemidorus' example is (IV. 24): A sick man dreams about an old woman, then dies. This is how it is worked out:

old woman	=	γ	ρ	α	ῦ	ς				(*graus*)
numerical values	=	3	100	1	400	200				= 704

funeral	=	ἡ	ἐ	κ	φ	o	ρ	ά	(*he ekphora*)
numerical values	=	8	5	20	500	70	100	1	= 704

But then Artemidorus calmly adds in his matter-of-fact way that the adding up is not necessary, for an old woman indicates death anyway.

Here is one last example of this "isopsephisms" interpretation: (IV. 22): A man in Rome who is off on his travels asks someone in the dream whether he will return safely to Rome. The reply is "οὔ" = not; but the numerical value of οὔ is 470 (o = 70, υ = 400), so the real reply is after 470 days, which is actually what happened!

These speculations seem somewhat hazardous to us, but do we know the mathematics of the unconscious? Isn't extensive literature on "numerology" still much in use? And aren't Kabbalah speculations, and others, too, including Christian ones, full of such strange systems? One has only to think of astrology and the so-called Gematria. Correlations of this kind have been believed in India since time immemorial and have cosmogonic significance there (hierarchy of the conscious and the world = psyche). One should also look at Sir John Woodroffe, *The Garland of Letters* (Varnamala).[111] In Jungian terms this is all phenomenology of the unconscious, which also accounts for Jung's "On the Significance of Number Dreams,"[112] about which we still have a few misgivings today. When these correlations fit, then it is only with an above-average dose of intuition, which Jung says is accurate in 50 percent of the cases![113]

The reader will notice how much of the advice in Artemidorus' five books is still of value today. Unfortunately, his work was not accessible until a few years ago. The first reliable edition of the text came out in 1963 in the "Bibliotheca Teubneriana."[114] It took even longer for the German translation, for the one that was available was inadequate.[115] This may be the reason modern psychologists have a poor opinion of Artemidorus, although Freud went into him very thoroughly. For our purposes, the translation by Krauss was the only one available.[116]

(d) Dream Oracle and Incubation

We have seen that in Ancient Greece dreams were regarded as genuine oracles. Unlike other well-known methods of seeking oracles—such as auguries, haruspicies, etc., which all have a fixed reference system with a limited number of possible answers—the dream has no such fixed pattern. Because it is so polymorphous its interpretation called for greater depth of experience and knowledge, or else, which was actually the case, it leads to a quite superficial and cheap schematism.

This difficulty may have contributed to the fact that early on the Greeks viewed the dream in a special way, regarding it as an *oracle on sickness and healing*. This specialization meant that two adaptations were called for: (1) one had to be able to turn to a god who was also specialized in this sphere and a corresponding cult had to be set up for him, and (2) it had to be a chthonic divinity to whom one turned, as body and earth were practically synonymous. In this connection the ancient belief that the "Mistress of the Earth" (*πότνια Χθῶν, potnia Chthon*) was the mother of all dreams was both meaningful and useful.

Chthonic gods are tied to their specific abode, so that one has to make an effort, a pilgrimage to go to them. With the passage of time and the countless number of pilgrimages, the shrine acquires great prestige and mana. There were archaic models for this type of dream oracle, e.g., in the cave shrines of the chthonic heroes Amphiaraos and Trophonios, who had always answered questions or performed miraculous cures. Furthermore, there was an old mythological doctor, Asclepius, who was later elevated to divinity.

Such heroes or gods who had specialized in medicine had, of course, been found in many different races and cultures, but none of them could compete with Asclepius. As far as we can make out, his cult was also distinctive in the way it was carried out. I shall now attempt to give a very brief description of the ritual in the shrines of Asclepius, in other words, what the so-called practice of *incubation* consists of. I refer the reader to my more detailed description in "Ancient Incubation and Modern Psychotherapy,"[117] which contains comparative material on Trophonius, Amphiaraos, Kalchas, Faunus, Isis and Sarapis. Here we must do the reverse and take Asclepius as *pars pro toto*, and similarly I will confine myself solely to Epidauros as the most famous of all the Asclepieia (shrines or sanctuaries of Asclepius).

Epidauros is splendidly situated in an inland valley of Argolis; it is connected to the harbor of the same name by a 5-mile long *via sacra*. Its buildings were famous in the ancient world for their beauty, especially its theatre and the round temple, the *tholos*. The sacred precinct is teeming with harmless snakes and there are many magnificent oriental plane trees. There was also a lot of water. Next to the entrance there are six steles on which are carved over one hundred medical case histories, which are striking evidence of its reputation. Some seventy of them are preserved, and are accessible in an exemplary edition by Rudolf Herzog.[118]

As a patient one was allowed into the sacred precinct without further ado, except if one was moribund or pregnant and about to give birth, for the shrine had to be kept ritually pure of death and birth. After certain purification rites, ablutions and provisional sacrifices had been performed, one was allowed to sleep there, on what was known as a "Kline" (κλίνη), a word from which our term clinic is descended. The dormitory was called Abaton or Adyton, the literal meaning of which is "the room that must not be entered by the uninvited." From this phrase we can conclude that in Epidaurus, too, it was a mystery cult, for it is a *locus communis* for those who were designated or called to the initiation (for example, see what Apuleius has to say about the Isis mysteries).

The question of whether or not one was "designated" was probably answered by what happened during the earlier performing of the sacrifices. Once one was admitted, everything else depended on whether one had the *right* dream while asleep in the Abaton. This is what the word "incubation" actually means, for *"incubare"* simply means "sleeping in the shrine," expressed in Greek by the expression ἐγκοίμησις (*enkoimesis*). The dormitory in the sacred precinct is also called Enkoimeterion, which is where cimitero (Italian) and cimetière (French) comes from. Whether the dream was the right one or not was decided by its effect, for in positive cases the patient woke up cured, which is why one is justified in speaking of "healing sleep."

Apparently dreams in which Asclepius appeared were always curative. The epiphany of the god could happen in two ways: either ὄναρ (*onar* = in the dream), or ὕπαρ (*hypar* = in the waking state), i.e., as a vision, probably when the incubant was too excited and could not sleep. The god either came alone, as the bearded man of his cult image, or as a youth. But often he was accompanied by his chaste wife or daughter Hygieia or by Jaso and Panacea. Instead of appearing in person he can also content himself with delegating one of these acolytes or his assistants Machaon and Podaleinos. But he also appears in his theriomorphous form, i.e., as a snake or a dog. He then touches the affected part of the patient's body and vanishes. In the early period of this cult, the patient was probably regarded as incurable if he did not experience a dream epiphany in the very first night, which apparently also meant that he was "not designated." Later this was decided by the outcome of the earlier sacrifices so that those seeking help often waited till the signs were favorable, i.e., when the καιρὸς ὀξύς (*kairos oxys*), the decisive moment occurred. In this way, as time went on, Epidauros became a large sanatorium.

But this development also had another, purely religious aspect: Normally the ex-patient seems to have gone away with a deep faith

in the power and the goodness of the god; through this experience
he had become a "religiosus," as the technical term went. This certainly plays a significant role for the lasting effect of the cure. It
was not necessary for the patient to become a "*fanaticus*," i.e., unable to tear himself away from the "*fanum*" (sacred precinct), but
a healthy transference (= *religiosus*) seems to have had very favorable effects. But there are cases where the patient stayed for a long
time in the secret precinct; this recalls the institute of the κατοχή
(*Katochè*), which had become famous through the shrines of the
most successful of Asclepius' colleagues, Sarapis. His κατοχοί
(*Katochoi*), i.e., voluntary temple prisoners, waited for a very long
time in these theurgical clinics. One of the most prominent of the
habitués of the many Asclepieia was the rhetorician Aelius Aristides
of Smyrna. Another famous man, Apuleius, described himself as
a captive (δέσμιος, *desmios*) of the goddess Isis.

As can be seen, there was no need for any dream interpreters at
such places. Moreover, there were no doctors, nor was medicine actually practiced. However, those seeking help were obliged to write
down their dreams, or have them written down. Aristides tells us
that the "prisoners" carefully wrote down their dreams until a
σύμπτωμα (symptom) occurred, i.e., a coinciding with the dream of
the priest. In another passage, he reveals that on occasion the priest
with whom he lodged outside the Hieron (shrine) or even his slave,
dreamt on his behalf. There is no other way of understanding this
except to imagine that the whole atmosphere of the Asclepieion must
have been permeated with a "healthful spirit."

In actual fact we find in the writings of Democritus, Aristotle and
Hippocrates listed earlier a sort of theoretical premise for this
method of observation. Apuleius aptly sums up the imprisonment
during the Isis mysteries as follows: "*neque vocatus morari, nec non
iussus festinare*" (Do not hesitate when called, but do not rush when
not commanded) and the day on which he was called to the initiation was "*divino vadimonio destinatus*" (defined by divine pledge).
Sometimes a quite specific vision was required, as a sign that the
petitioner was ready for the initiation, which apparently corresponded to the condition described at the Asclepiea as ἐνύπνιον ἐναργές (*enhypnion enarges*), the effective dream from which one woke up
cured. Once he was healed, the ex-patient was expected to pay a
small fee to the temple and to offer a sacrifice of thanksgiving. We
know of cases where the god taught a painful lesson by causing
relapses if people went into debt or if, after the cure, they lapsed
back into their old rationalism and scepticism, instead of becoming "*religiosi*."

From Plato's "Statesman" (III. 14.15) we can see what absolute authority the dream decisions of Asclepius had. He refuses to cure people who are not law-abiding, as they were of no use to society. On the other hand, there were patients who seem to have had a jovial relationship with the divine doctor, very reminiscent of the modern dialectical view of psychotherapy. There are some delightful anecdotes: a certain Polemon (in Philostratus), forbidden by Asclepius to drink water, replied: "What would you have prescribed for a cow?" or one Plutarch, recommended to eat pork, said: "What would you have ordered a Jew?" Asclepius took such jokes in good part and even sometimes changed his instructions.

But if it was a question of healing by paradoxes, i.e., when the very thing that was forbidden was the remedy, there was no arguing with him, even if the cure meant breaking a taboo, for example when a Greek Adonis worshipper had to eat raw boar meat. So the allopathic principle of *"contraria contrariis curentur"* is just as common as the homeopathic one of *"similia similibus."* The idea of the god actually issuing medical instructions is a feature that appeared only toward the end of the epoch; but in the ancient world already it was abused as an "aetiological myth" for the origins of the art of medicine. It was even claimed that Hippocrates had copied his therapy and wealth of medical knowledge from the archives of the temple cures in the Asclepieum of Kos. The shrine at Kos, as we know today, however, was founded after the death of Hippocrates, yet it was his students who felt it necessary to call additionally upon the divine doctor, in other words, felt that purely rational medicine did not fulfill all their needs.

The symbolism that built up over the years around the mystery of the healing in the cult in the Asclepieia has striking parallels with those in other mystery cults. For example, the healing was viewed as a rebirth. It was brought about by making contact with the element of the Earth in its divine aspect. Thus in all the Asclepieia, Demeter and Zeus Katachthonios (the underground one) are worshipped along with Asclepius and his father Apollo. In both the mythology and the cult of Asclepius there is a union of opposites. Apollo and his art, music and theatre play a prominent role in all the Asclepieia, which tells us that the *"cura animae"* was practiced in these ancient clinics and that they must have realized that the real object of the therapy is the "cult of the soul."

The combination of water, tree, snake, art, music, theatre and a chthonic cult whose high point occurred every night in a dream, i.e., in a highly personal experience, strikes me as going a long way toward accounting for the miraculous effects. At any rate, a lot

more was done for the soul here than we find at any modern sanatorium, be it a university clinic or Lourdes. Moreover, the most famous of the over 200 Asclepieia in the ancient world, such as
Epidauros, Kos, Pergamon and Athens, are all situated in a coun-
tryside of exquisite beauty, which must be taken into account as an
important fact in the creation of harmony between macrocosmos
and microcosmos; from the philosophical point of view, this harmony was, for the Greeks, a prerequisite for health.

It is in the same spirit that we have to understand that in the ancient world illness was identified with poverty (πενία, *penia*), just
as today we still ask our patients in German "Was *fehlt* Ihnen?"
There is nothing surprising about the fact that this abundance of
symbols in the Asclepius cult lent itself to converting this poverty
into wealth (πλοῦτος, *ploutous*), which in turn, is synonymous with
healing, health, holiness, wholeness—all expressions with close
etymological links. And so the illness became its own remedy,
offered by a god who had been a patient himself, but as a god was
able to overcome the illness, for he knew the remedy and was thus
able to pass it on to other patients through his divine intervention.

When we bear all this in mind, it becomes clear that Epidauros
was jealously intent on preserving its strict cultish tradition, making the founding of other Asclepieia dependent upon their descent
from Epidauros. Transferring the cult to a new center was naturally made to depend on transporting one of the Epidauros snakes
to the shrine that was to be founded. This made impossible the
phenomenon that is regrettably common in medicine or analytical
schools whereby colleagues obsessed with personal prestige vainly
lay claim to being the only representative and possessor of the true
spirit of their master.

Incubation, to me, is just *one* manifestation of something that can
be perceived by anyone who comes to Greece with his eyes open.
The whole country is still permeated by myth, and the ancient gods
are still present wherever you go. You only have to take a map of
Greece in one hand, and the "Baedeker" of Pausanias in the other
(preferably Frazer's edition with commentary) to see that you really
do have the geography of the human soul before you; not the Greek
one, not the Western one, but the human soul pure and simple. All
over this peninsula and its islands we come across hundreds of
shrines, each with its own special myth, its own special cult, its own
special cult legends and its temple, where one or other of the fundamental human problems was dealt with, in every possible variation, in great abundance, beauty and wholesomeness. Anyone
needing help in those days knew exactly where to turn, i.e., where

the appropriate archetype was presented and performed as befitted the cult.

We mentioned at the beginning why we are going into such detail with the Greek-Roman tradition. We hope that the reader has found much that he considers worth heeding. We are living in a culture that has its rules in Greek-Roman antiquity. What we found with Macrobius, namely that his influence was a long-lasting one, also applies to areas whose sources we have lost, the difference being that in these cases the tradition proceeds unconsciously. This does not mean that it loses in authenticity. For example, the many so-called "Egyptian Dream Books" which are still widely popular today are based entirely on Artemidorus in their dream-reality dictionary, and are often actual literal translations from the Oneirocritica.

I should like to offer evidence of the fact that tradition often proceeds in an unconscious manner. Schopenhauer writes:

> But as we fall asleep, when external impressions cease to function and the alertness of the thoughts within the sensorium gradually fade away, then there will become perceptible those weak impressions that immediately rise to the surface from within the nerve mass of organic life, just like any slight modification in the blood circulation which affects the vessels in the brain; it is like when a candle seems to burn brightly as twilight falls, or the way we hear a spring running at night when it is drowned by the noise of the day. Impressions that are much too weak to affect the brain when it is awake and active are able, once the brain has stopped its own activity, to produce a gentle agitation of its individual parts and their powers of fantasy; it is like a harp that will only resound with an external echo when it is just hanging there, but not when it is being played itself. So the dream figures that emerge as we fall asleep must have their origins here, and this is what makes it possible to define them more clearly. This is just as true of the dreams that arise out of the absolute mental repose, of deep sleep with their dramatic continuity. The only thing is that as these dreams occur when the brain is perfectly at rest and given over to its nutrition, a significantly stronger impulse from within is called for. That is precisely why it is just these dreams which in individual, very rare cases, have a prophetic or fatidical meaning, and Horace is right when he says: *post mediam noctem, cum somnia vera.*[119]

This should be compared with what we summed up about Aristotle's view earlier. The striking parallels make me think of a case of cryptomnesia (cf. Vol. I of this textbook), as Schopenhauer is generally very conscientious about giving his sources.

Anyone wishing to make use of the *scriptores minori* to get more detailed information about dreams from the Greek world will find the extensive collection of Darius del Corno[120] extremely useful.

4. Late Antiquity, the Middle Ages and the Renaissance

The scholarly discussion of dreams did not, of course, cease as the period of classical antiquity drew to a close. But in the Middle Ages there seem to be no more summary works on the subject. St. Augustine studied dreams, but his interest lies mainly in distinguishing between dreams as divine revelations and dreams as diabolic illusions. In the 12th century John of Salisbury made a detailed observation of dreams in his "Polycraticus."[121] Albertus Magnus (1193–1280) adheres to the distinction between "dreams from God" and "natural dreams," and in this he is followed by his disciples Thomas Aquinas (1227–1274) and Vincenz de Beauvais (–– 1250). With the Spaniard Arnaldus de Villanova (1235–1312) we find, perhaps for the first time, the view often put forward as the physical stimulus theory. Tommaso Campanella (1568–1639) then ascribes dreaming to the working of the world soul, as do all Renaissance philosophers. During this period the paths followed are Neoplatonist or Plotinian, although people did enjoy arguing with the philosophies of Iamblichus and Proclus.

Unfortunately, neither the above nor many other authors from the time between late antiquity and the Renaissance have been examined about their attitude toward dreams. An even more serious gap exists from the 16th to the 18th century. In his autobiographical book *Somniorum Synesiorum,*[122] Cirolamo Cardano, one of the most eminent of Renaissance scholars, gives us a remarkable insight into the role of the dream.

5. The Romantic Age and Modern Times

A striking revival of interest in the dream occurred in the Romantic Age. This revaluation of the dream can be seen most clearly in Romantic *poets* such as Novalis, Jean Paul, Herder and Tieck. But the *philosophers* of the 18th century also took a new interest in the manifestations of the unconscious and hence the dream. Interestingly enough, Leibniz (1646–1716) may actually be regarded as a forerunner in this respect. In his theory of monads the term "unconscious" crops up for the first time in history as far as we can see. He talks of "petites perception," i.e., changes in the soul which we are not aware of as they are too weak or too numerous, and describes them as consciousness differentials, which are conscious for themselves alone and which he thus describes as "perceptions insensible." They produce images of the sensory attributes which are still muddled in their individual parts.

With Kant (1724-1804), in "Anthropology" and in the "Critique of Judgment," we read: "The field of dark ideas is very large," and on the subject of dreams we learn that they come from the involuntary agitations of the internal life organs, that they have life-giving force and that there is "no sleep without dream." Note how close these observations are to modern sleep and dream research.

Let us now have a look at a Swiss philosopher, Ignaz Paul Vital Troxler (Beromünster 1780, --Bern 1866), a very interesting man who has never been given the credit he deserves. Troxler was a doctor (we come back in a moment to the role of the doctor in this discussion), and as a philosopher was a disciple of Schelling. (We know that Schelling was friendly with Novalis.) Troxler[122] writes aphorisms of a genuinely Romantic character, such as this one: "Waking is a dream of the soul," and Eschenmayer[123] quotes him as follows:

> The dream is the very reason for waking and sleeping. Waking is a dream of the soul, sleep a dream of the body. The dream is the expression of the absolute relationship of mind and body, waking and sleeping are just relative relationships of soul and body. The dream is man's innate, original source, of which waking and sleeping are just modifications.

As can be seen, we have here, as with Nietzsche, a "re-evaluation of all values."

Johann Karl Friedrich Rosenkranz (1805-1879) deals with the dream problem in a very interesting way in his "Psychologie oder die Wissenschaft vom subjektiven Geist."[124] Rosenkranz is a disciple of Hegel. For him, as with Troxler, the dream is the unity of sleeping and waking, actually the being awake in sleep, an existence of the one in the other. We are automatically reminded here of the "paradoxical" features of REM sleep (see above). Troxler goes on to say that in dream life the subject of the mind (the conscious) is resolved into an indefinite objectivity, which strikes me as particularly modern, for an objectifying effect of the dream leads quite logically to its interpretation on the subjective level in Jungian terms.

We have already quoted Schopenhauer, but in his Parerga and Paralipomena there are further assertions that are of interest to us: the dream comes from internal organic stimuli (sympathetic nervous system). The dream organ is an intuitive faculty, independent of external stimuli. The ego is the clandestine theatre director of dreams (Transcendental Speculation on the apparent Intentionality in the Destiny of the Individual). In dreams everyone is a Shakespeare.

We touch here on the thorny question of the responsibility for dreams and, as we have already mentioned, on the Jungian principle of the interpretation on the subjective level.

In his *Psychologie*[125] J. H. Fichte (1797–1879), the younger Fichte and son of the famous Johann Gottlieb Fichte, devotes a lot of space to fantasy and dream, especially in Part 1, III.3. He explains that fantasy is the dream-forming faculty (cf. Synesius) and that it is always awake and at work within us. The dream state is inferior to the conscious state, but also *richer and more interesting*, because hitherto unsuspected riches from the preconscious region can rise to the surface. Once again we recognize the regressive higher appreciation of the unconscious, which is so characteristic of the Romantic Age.

Gustav Theodor Fechner, to whom we referred in the first volume of this textbook, also shares this view, but from the philosophical point of view he is an objective idealist. For him the mind is the objective being (das "An-sich") of things. Any totality or existence has a soul. Let us remember that Fechner made this unusual metamorphosis from physicist to natural philosopher and mystic under the influence of what was probably a functional blindness. He sees the dreamer as a poet who gives free rein to his fantasy and is totally absorbed and lost in an inner world.

Let us now turn to the doctors and theologians of the Romantic Age and see what they have to say on this subject. One who achieved world fame is Franz Anton Mesmer (1734–1815) whose method of "magnetic sleep" with the aid of "animal magnetism" was an exciting innovation all over Europe. Despite its questionable scientific character, it led to a large number of reputed authors beginning to give serious consideration to the phenomenon of sleep and dreaming, which was part of the Romantic movement, with its emphasis on man's night side, i.e., the soul.

The doctor, natural scientist and theologian Gotthilf Heinrich von Schubert (Erlangen, 1780–1860) was a passionate advocate of the soul and became famous through his two main works "Die Symbolik des Traumes" (1813) and "Die Geschichte der Seele" (1830). He was a disciple of Herder and Schelling and was admired by Goethe and Jean Paul. In turn he influenced the Schlegel brothers, Kleist and E.T.A. Hoffmann. He was also interested in Mesmer's magnetism. There is still a lot to be gained from reading his works today, but we just quote two statements relevant to our subject:

1. Germs of new life are slumbering in us and emerge in our dreams.

2. "The nocturnal depth of our being" i.e., the dream, must be studied under a microscope.

Carl Gustav Carus (1831–1866), a famous doctor in his day, was also a prolific writer and was friendly with Goethe. In his work "Psyche" we find the much-quoted sentence: "The key to recognizing the essence of the conscious soul life lies in the region of the unconscious." In the same place we find the following remark: "The whole world of our innermost spiritual being reposes in the unconscious and works its way out from there." His "Symbolik der menschlischen Gestalt" (1852) represents, among other things, a true forerunner of modern psychosomatic medicine, which is unjustifiably forgotten today. A few quotations from his "Vorlesungen über Psychologies, gehalten im Winter 1829/30 in Dresden"[126] will show in what perspective Carus views dreams and how close he comes to modern findings:

> If it emerged from our earlier observation on the development of the soul that with regard to development we have to distinguish mainly between two conditions, namely the unconscious and the conscious state of the soul, the latter also being divided into world-consciousness and self-consciousness, and if we also noted that these two states did not follow each other, with one cancelling out the other, but that the higher one penetrated into the inferior one that remained, and unfolded itself, and that the soul then led a double life, an unconscious and a conscious one at the same time, then it will be understood how and why the more freely developed soul will still persist in fluctuating between these two poles, like in a night life and a day life, now with proposals from the conscious and now with proposals from the unconscious state.[127]

In the XIV. Lecture Carus deals at length with sleep as a repetition of the unconscious primitive state of man in the life before birth, and designates the dream as the continuation of an existence in an apparent nonexistence, as one of the strangest phenomena in the sphere of psychology. In the XV. Lecture he treats dreaming as the activation of the conscious within the soul which has returned to the sphere of the unconscious. He distinguishes three types of dreams: (a) insignificant, (b) portentous and (c) clairvoyant. Of the last-mentioned he says that they bear testimony to the far-reaching link between the supreme life in Nature and mankind, a link which with changes of inner disposition can be perceived according to features which we have no notion of in a normal state.

There were understandably great outpourings of literature on the dream in the Romantic Age, as can be seen from the bibliographies of Freud[128] and Von Siebenthal.[129] But they have nothing new to say, compared to the works already referred to, so we shall just briefly mention the most important contributions.

The theologian Franz Splittengerber brought out a book *Sleep and Death*[130] in 1865; let us recall that Hypnos (sleep) and Thanatos (death) are brothers in ancient mythology, and that this link is often the reason why some people have difficulty in falling asleep. Purkinje[131] quotes a Greek writer of gnomic poetry who calls sleep a preparatory exercise for death (θάνατος τὶς προμελέτησις, *thanatos tis promeletesis*) or a small death mystery (ὕπνος τὰ μικρὰτοῦ θάνατον μυστήρια, *hypnos ta mikratou thanatou mysteria*). This writer is Mnesimachos.[132] The "small mysteries" which were celebrated in Agrai in March were known to be a prerequisite for participating in the great Eleusinian mysteries in September.

The philosopher Heinrich Spitta published a book in 1877 on the sleep and dream states of the human soul[133] in which he regards the absence of self-consciousness as the essential modulator of the dream.

The last author to be mentioned in this group is Paul Radestock[134] with his book *Sleep and Dream*. He is a product of the essentially physiologically oriented school of W. Wundt and therefore claims the "ceasing of thinking" as the main modulator of the dream.

The reader who wishes to have a more comprehensive picture of this epoch is recommended to turn to the works of Philipp Lersch[135] and Albert Béguin.[136]

6. Dream Theory in Modern Times

The English ophthalmologist and neurologist John Hughlings Jackson[137] (London, 1834–1911) had a marked influence on Freud with his scientific approach toward the links between psychology and physiology, as has been proved by Ola Andersson.[138] This is particularly true of the Breur-Freudian theory of abreacting. Jackson's works have been made more easily accessible by a new edition,[139] the most interesting ones for us being his Croonian lectures of 1884,[140] "Evolution and Dissolution of the Nervous System." On the basis of clinical observation of people with brain damage, Jackson concludes that there is a hierarchical system in the structure of the central nervous system, and believes that to a large extent it goes parallel with the structure of the psychic functions, or vice-versa. He talks of a principle of "progressive cerebration." (Perhaps it is worth stating that this view has been largely confirmed by the research of the Zurich physiologist and Nobel prizewinner W. R. Hess and recent neuro-psychological findings, especially regarding primitive vegetative functions.)

Jackson then explains that in the dream, as in psychoses, there is a sinking of the psychic functions to a lower structural level, and that at the same time there is an increased physiological activity of normal nervous arrangements on the structural level that remains. The lower structural level, which is in greater physiological activity in the dream, allows for a wider irradiation of the simple impulses which reach it. Once again we recall the views of Aristotle (see above). On account of its psychological interest we quote an excerpt from Jackson's writings:

> We develop as we must, that is, according to what we are by inheritance; and also as we can, that is, according to external conditions. There is something more: there is what I will call Internal Evolution, a process which goes on most actively in the highest centers. On account of its great preponderance in the highest centers of man, he differs so greatly from lower animals. We acquire numerous different ideas: that is to say, there is, on the physical side, an organization of many different nervous arrangements of our highest centers, during actual converse with the environment. When, as in sleep and in "reflection," this actual converse ceases, the quasi-spontaneous slight activity of the highest sensory centers is uninterfered with by the environment, they being protected from it by the lowest and middle sensory centers; and, consequently, there are no reactions on the environment, the highest motor center being resisted by the middle and lowest centers; in such case (sleep, reverie, reflection, etc.), the very highest nervous arrangements of the highest centers, those in which entirely new organizations can be made, will be in least activity, and the next lower of those centers in greater activity. The nervous arrangements of the highest centers, or some elements of them, are "left to fight it out among themselves"; new combinations arise, the survival of the fittest. Manifestly new, although, evanescent combinations, are made during dreaming; but I contend that permanent rearrangements (internal evolutions) are made during so-called dreamless sleep.[141]

Pierre Janet (Paris, 1859–1947) operates in the same way with notions of "psychic levels" and his works on the subject were of great value to Jung, especially for his doctrine of complexes (see Vol. I of this textbook).

In his monograph "L'état mental des hystériques"[142] Janet first introduces the notion of "niveau mental." The height of this level, he claims, is in negative correlation to the emotional excitement, so that with strong emotion there is an "abaissement du niveau mental." In a later work,[143] instead of using the vague expression "niveau mental," Janet speaks more precisely of "tension psychologique." What he says is based on purely clinical observations, although unlike Jackson he is not interested in the localisatory questions in the CNS. His views should be seen clearly in the following two quotations:

> Pour résumer cette curieuse observation nous pouvons dire que nous avons assisté à une modification remarquable de tout l'esprit sous l'influence d'une émotion. En présence des discussions actuelles sur le caractère de l'émotion, il était intéressant de constater ces changements et leur évolution. Une théorie qui a longtemps régné admettait comme phénomène essentiel de l'émotion des troubles viscéraux; ceux-ci ont existé probablement au début, ils n'ont pas été bien considérables et ils n'ont pas duré longtemps. A côté d'eux nous voyons beaucoup d'autres phénomènes d'agitation musculaire et mentale, les convulsions et les délires. Mais ce qui a été le principal, ce qui domine toutes ces agitations, c'est l'abaissement du niveau mental, la diminution de toutes les opérations supérieures de volonté, d'attention, d'assimilation personnelle.[144]
>
> La notion de l'abaissement de la tension psychologique est un des meilleurs résumés que l'on puisse donner de l'état de l'esprit pendant le sommeil.[145]

It is actually possible to look at a series of more or less abnormal psychic states from this point of view, for example depression, excitation, sentiment d'incomplétude, but also the occurrence of automatisms which then, corresponding more to another "niveau" theory of Janet's, would be attributed to the predominance of the "fonction inférieure d'adaptation" (as opposed to the "fonctions supérieures"). Generally speaking, what we are dealing with here is a special form of the libido theory, which has certain points in common with that of Jung, to which we shall return later.

According to Janet's views, sleep is a regular, rhythmic and normally occurring oscillation downwards of the "niveau mental."

CHAPTER IV

THE DREAM IN C.G. JUNG'S COMPLEX PSYCHOLOGY

Was von Menschen nicht gewusst
Oder nicht bedacht
Durch das Labyrinth der Brust
Wandelt in der Nacht.[146]
    —Goethe, 1778
    "An dem Mond"

1. Complex Theory and Dream

Through Jung's discovery of and research into the complex, the whole psychoanalytical school was given vital support and at the time it was *de facto* only on the basis of this that it gained access into the world of academic psychology and psychiatry. The historical foundations for this state of affairs have been dwelt on at length in the first volume of this textbook. The complex theory also proved to be exceptionally productive for the dream theory. We briefly recapitulate here what we have learned from the complex theory:

The so-called "feeling-toned complex" is a content of the psyche which leads a sort of separate existence in the psychic structure of its bearer; it is split off or "sandwiched in," as they used to say. It is always "feeling-toned," either positively or negatively, and it is precisely because of this feeling tone that it is relatively incompatible with the conscious. Because of this incompatibility it remains separate from the psychic structure and thus becomes autonomous,

i.e., it makes its presence felt spontaneously, especially as a disturbance or a compulsion. Complexes are almost like living organisms
in that they assimilate other psychic contents and hence increase in
dimension. The contents assimilated obviously have some sort of
associative connection with the central elements of the complex.
This ability of the complex to assimilate means that in pathological cases it can even turn into partial personalities of the subject; that
is when we speak of split personalities or part personalities. On a
small scale this is even the case with a healthy person who has, as
it were, his compartments, the contents of which have little or no
connection with each other (compartment psychology). On this
topic Jung usually told the story of the English parson committed
for stealing from the poorbox, who denied it, saying: "But a parson does not steal." Such partial personalities have also been
produced in the experimental situation, by Morton Prince[147] for example, who succeeded in producing up to four such part personalities with his test subjects, each of which was totally different and
knew nothing of the other.

This reminds us of the belief of primitive peoples that all people
have a number of souls, and that it can easily happen that one goes
astray, which is then described as "soul loss," a state which with
us would correspond to something like depression. It is interesting
to see what sort of therapy the primitives resort to in such situations:
the lost soul has to be recaptured. So the medicine man goes off to
catch birds—it is not only with the Greeks that the soul is a bird.
When he returns with his cage full of birds, the patient is laid on the
ground and starting from his head a 2-metre-long line of grains of
seed is laid down, at the end of which the birds are set free. One
of them, which of course is regarded as the soul bird of the patient,
sets about pecking at the grains and finally arrives at the patient's
head. The last grain has been placed on the top of his head and
when it is eaten, it is assumed that the bird has "returned" to the
patient and has thus cured him.

The "voices" of schizophrenics should also be viewed in the same
light as the theory of complexes, as should many externally projected
manifestations, such as elves, green folks and brownies. The fact
that this projection of the complex occurs automatically also leads
to the denouncing of circumstances and objects. Examples of such
"cussedness of things" can be found in F.Th. Vischer's novel *Auch
Einer*. Complexes can have a contagious effect on others, a situation which emerges most clearly between members of the same
family, and has broken up many a family with its violent accompanying emotional outbursts. When a complex has accumulated so

much further material that even the ego of the subject is assimilated by it, this brings about a change in personality, i.e., a complex identity. Its clinical manifestation ranges from relatively harmless neurosis to actual obsession (examples of this can be seen in Aldous Huxley's book *The Devils of Loudun*).

In view of all these shattering effects, the phrases "it's just a complex" should not be bandied around too loosely. It remains a dangerous *corpus alienum* in the organism, and its effects are constantly felt. For example, when it is somewhat stimulated by some external or internal "complex irritation," it can bring about unpleasant disturbances of the memory. It is characteristic of such effects that they can appear in two totally different forms, for example, either in simply forgetting or else in obstinately clinging to certain ideas, in other words obsessions. The accompanying physical effects that this affect gives rise to also have this ambivalence so that the same complex irritation can trigger off blushing or going pale, sweating or one's hair standing on end, etc.

I have already dwelt at length in Vol. I of this textbook on the various accompanying physical effects of complexes and their emotional tone. Let us merely recall here that language has many figures of speech to express this, and this is particularly true of dream language. Examples are: "to lose one's tongue," when "one's heart beats faster" or "stands still" or "breaks," "to have something on one's chest," and there are many more.

Aldous Huxley describes a case of physical effects so accurately that I quote it here:

> In the course of his strange career, Surin was alternatively strangled and released, locked up in stifling darkness and transported to a mountain top in the sun. And his lungs reflected the state of his soul—cramped and rigid when the soul was stifled, dilated when it drew breath. The words serré, bandé, rétréci, and their antithesis, dilaté, recur again and again in Surin's writings. They express the cardinal fact of his experience—a violent oscillation between the extremes of tension and release, of a contraction into less than self and a letting go into more abundant Life.[148]

It was exactly 30 years (1934) after his great discovery (1904) that Jung first dealt with the significance of the complex for dream research in a publication,[149] although he had of course been making use of what he wrote there ever since the early days. The conclusion he reaches, which is important for us, is that complexes appear in personified forms in dreams, that their being and effects are activated there to a certain extent, and are presented in "dramatic form," and that the dream is thus a self-representation of the complex. In the dream the complexes frequently take over that activity that falls to the conscious ego in the waking state. They thus have a certain egoishness, which gives rise to the question of whether they have their own consciousness even if it is only a partial one. This then brings up the whole problem of the freedom of the ego with its thorny question of the responsibility for dreams. (The reader is reminded here of Schopenhauer's two remarks on pp. 77–78, and also the fact that even St. Augustine wrestled with this problem.) More on this subject later.

Let us now attempt to present in more detail Jung's view of the significance of the theory of complexes for the dream theory:

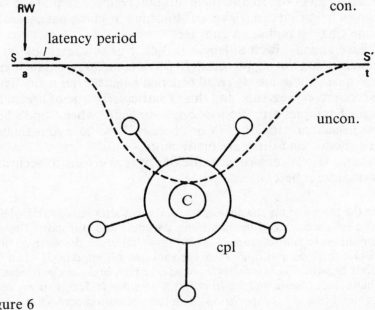

Figure 6

Let us assume that the line S–S′ in Fig. 6 indicates the consciousness threshold; above it there is consciousness whereas everything below it belongs to the unconscious. In the unconscious the complexes are to be found, some close to the consciousness threshold, others deeper down. Let us further assume that S–S′ is also the time axis; a complex irritation is set at time point a from outside, i.e., the complex is stimulated, ionized to a certain extent, e.g., through a complex stimulus word, so that it becomes "electrically" active. Experimental and clinical experience shows that after a certain latency period of about one second, the S–S' threshold sinks and the complex thus lands in the sphere of the conscious, which amounts to a penetrating of the unconscious. (Let us recall here Janet's *oscillation du niveau mental*, as well as the comments in Vol. I of this textbook.)

As a caption to Fig. 6, it must be noted that with the complex we indicate the so-called nuclear element of the complex with the small circle, whereas the large concentric circle indicates the range of the complex. This is why it is much larger than the nucleus, because in the course of time the last-mentioned has assimilated further material from the related feeling tone. The satellite circles are meant to indicate contents that are initially loosely associated with the complex but which, in the course of time, if the complex is given the opportunity to continue its growth unimpeded, are merged with the shell, i.e., are assimilated.

The state that is brought about through the temporary *abaissement du niveau mental* always has an emotional tone, and it is this in particular that continues to vibrate afterwards, i.e., outlasts the other effects of the complex and also has attendant somatic symptoms.

These remarks on the effects of complexes should make it easier to understand Jung's view that dream figures are personifications of complexes. For what we have here with the effect of a complex irritation in the Association Experiment is the normal in sleep in that the level S–S' in this natural state of the unconscious sinks *physiologically*, so that the complexes become visible and dramatically active in personified form.

2. Dramatic Structure of the Dream

The above line of reasoning about the theory of complexes leads logically to a further recommendation by Jung, one which has proved of great value in actual practice, and that is to understand the dream as a "drame intérieur." The structure and course of the dream would then be similar to the structure of drama, drama in its ancient traditional form. We recall that Schopenhauer calls every dreamer a Shakespeare and makes him the "*Theatre* director" of his dreams. This is where the romantic view that the dream is the origin of poetry and drama has its place. Although Jung published these first findings in 1945,[150] he had been making use of them for more than twenty years.

Let us assume that the structure of classical drama is something like this:

1. Indication of place, time and dramatis personae.
2. Exposition (δέσις, *desis*), i.e., initial situation, involvement, weaving of the plot.
3. Peripetia (κρίσις, *krisis* = decision) or culmination, dramatic climax, crucial events, presentation of transformation (possible catastrophe).
4. Solution (λύσις, *lysis*), meaningful conclusion, result.

Let us now go through a dream divided up by Jung in this way in the work mentioned above:

1. I am in a simple house with a farmer's wife.
2. I tell her about a long journey to Leipzig.
3. On the horizon there appears a monstrous crab, which is also a saurian and which sort of gets me in its claws.
4. Miraculously, I have in my hand a divining rod and I touch the head of the monster with it. It collapses and dies.

To avoid giving the impression that this is just coincidence, let us look at another example from Jung:[151]

1. I am on a street, it is an avenue.
2. In the distance a car appears, approaching rapidly. It is being driven rather unsteadily and I think the driver must be drunk.
3. Suddenly, I am in the car and apparently I myself am this drunken driver. But I am not drunk, just oddly insecure and as if I have no steering-wheel. I cannot control the fast-moving car and crash into a wall.
4. I see that the front part of the car is smashed. It is a strange car that I do not know. I myself am unhurt. I think with some uneasiness of my responsibility.

For our third example let us look at how the initial dream of a depressive patient (p. 8) fits into this schema.

1. I was fishing for trout, not in an ordinary river or lake but in a reservoir, which was divided up into various compartments.
2. I was using ordinary fishing tackle (flies, etc.). I was having no luck.
3. As I was growing angry and impatient, I picked up a trident that was lying there
4. and immediately caught a splendid fish.

It is obvious that there will be dreams that do not seem to fit into this schema. Personally, however, I must confess that since getting the idea from Jung I have come across remarkably few exceptions (we shall return later to one such exception). In private practice and in many seminars the method has proved itself hundred of times.

This idea of Jung's is worth looking at more closely for its deep significance.

Its first prerequisite is that the dream is a whole entity, with a beginning and an end. We side with Aristotle with his definition of wholeness, for in the Poetics (VII,3) he demands that a complete plot (τελείας πράξεως, *teleias praxeos*) should have a beginning, middle and end as the three constituent elements (τὸ ἔχον ἀρχὴν καὶ μέσον καὶ τελευτήν, *to echon archen kai meson kai teleuten*).

We are still talking about the presentation of a conflict and its solution (*lysis* = liberation, rescue) (δρᾶμα, *drama* = plot). If the presentation and solution of the conflict in the dream are to proceed so consistently, this would give rise to a very interesting question of a humanistic nature. For example, one could ask whether the schema of real drama is a pattern of behavior, inherent in the human psyche. This would be an archetypal structure, about which we shall talk more in the fourth volume. This would mean that drama has its origins in the dreams, which is what the Romantics had been saying.

If the dream brings a solution to the conflict, this would, in terms of ancient drama, sometimes appear as a *deus ex machina*. There seems to be an obvious case of this in the form of the divining rod in example 1. Another example that can be taken literally is the trident in the initial dream of our patient. Let us not belabor this to the point of absurdity, but let us still bear in mind the attitude toward dreams in ancient times, where the notoriously expected divine intervention is simply due to the fact that dreams are sent from God, which explains their divinatory character.

Anyone with clinical psychiatric experience cannot help being deeply impressed by the total extent to which these patients have become the *plaything of their complexes*, so much so that their very destinies are controlled by these complexes, for in many cases the problem goes right through the family for generations. Often there is no getting away from the argument of analogy with ancient tragedy. One has only to think of the curse of the Atrids. We do not mean this in any fatalistic sense but would simply recommend that the dramatically active complex personification of our dreams be seen against this background, too. How often do we wake up from such dreams and say with a sense of relief: only a dream, thank God!

It was Nietzsche[152] who pointed out that the oldest dramas were probably the Mystery plays. These plays always deal with a mythical event which has an exemplary character and thus becomes a "therapeutical myth." From our point of view, the Mystery plays showed one the best way to conduct oneself toward the complexes. So dreams are also sometimes worth looking at for their lytic effect. Nietzsche's statement[153] that in the dream we have to carry out the allotted tasks of earlier generations may also be seen in this light, for these nightly "drames intérieurs" are *typical* human situations which remain the same *mutatis mutandis* through all ages. This statement of Nietzsche does of course contain the beginning of Jung's theory of the *collective unconscious*, to which we shall return in Volume IV.

What we still have to look at closely in this context is the abovementioned (Chap. II. 4) question of the effectiveness of the dream as such.

In connection with the dramatic structure of the dream, we cannot avoid the "Poetics" of Aristotle, from which, with Jung, we have already borrowed the schema for the structure of the drama. In "Politics"[154] as well Aristotle treats the question of the *effectiveness of the drama*, which I dealt with in my inaugural lecture at the E.T.H.[155] It would seem fitting to quote the most important passages here.

> By arousing pity and fear, tragedy brings about the alleviating discarding of such affects.
>
> —Aristotle, *Poetics* VI,2
> Translation by Bernays

Rightly in our view, Bernays translates πάθημα (*pathema*) with "affect" and χάθαϱσις (*Katharsis*) with "alleviating discarding."

Similar notions are at the basis of Plato's pronouncements (in: Leg. 791). Much has been written and there have been many arguments about the question of whether and on whom the dramatic performance should have the cathartic effect. One only needs to think of Lessing (77 plays) or Goethe (correspondence with Zelter and others). The argument was accepted or rejected according to temperament, for it is not easy to see who has correctly read the above words of Aristotle. At any rate, the discussion goes on for a long time. Adolf Stahr[156] and Adolph Silberstein[157] are names that come to mind.

It is to the credit of Jacob Bernays[158] that on the basis of strict philological and comparative arguments he has probably come up with the correct interpretation. In his view, the catharsis with Aristotle is a ἰατρεία (*iatreia*), i.e., a medical term. Experiencing a theatrical performance is supposed to make it possible for the spectator to get rid of his "anxiety" by helping him to have affective outbursts.

> Just as fire ignites when flammable material comes near to it, so a tragic plot consisting of sad and terrible events must arouse pity and terror in everyone, i.e., must bring about an outburst of these affects in any spectator in a natural frame of mind.[159]
>
> Catharsis is: a term indicating the shift from the physical to the emotional in the treating of someone who experiences anxiety, a treatment which does not try to transform or suppress the anxiety-causing element, but stimulates it, brings it to the fore and thus brings about relief for the person in question.[160]

In our language we would call it a discarding or discharging of the complex aroused by the plot or action, although for Aristotle there are just ἔλεος (*eleos*) and φόβος (*phobos*), pity and fear. As can be seen, this, too, is a sort of homeopathic medicine.[161] Milton (Samson Agonistes) reminds us of this aspect when he writes:

> Tragedy is said by Aristotle to be of power, by raising pity and fear, or terror, to purge the mind of those and such like passions, that is to temper and reduce them to just measure with a kind of delight, stirred up by reading or seeing those passions well imitated. Nor is Nature wanting in her own effects to make good his assertion: for so in physic things of melancholic hue and quality are used against melancholy, sour against sour, salt to remove salt humors.[162]

In connection with this, Bernays mentions St. Augustine (Conf. III,2), giving the following translation:

> . . . I happily allowed myself to be chained with agonizing bonds in order to be whipped with the glowing iron rods of jealousy, suspicion, anger and discord. I was fascinated by the stage, full as it was with the images of my sufferings and the tinder of my fire. What does it mean that Man wants to experience pain by looking at sad and tragic things which he would never want to have to put up with himself? And yet the spectator does want pain from this and it is precisely this pain that is his delight. What else can this be but sorrowful melancholia? For the emotion is all the stronger the more one suffers oneself from these urges, although if one suffers oneself it is called suffering, and if one shares in someone else's suffering it is called pity. But what sort of pity can it be when there are fabricated stage

conditions? The spectator is not called upon to give support but is invited to share pain; the stronger the pain, the more applause the one presenting these images receives. And if these wretched destinies, which have long disappeared or faded away, were presented in such a way that the spectator did not feel any pain, he would go away bored and dissatisfied; but if it hurts, he remains attentive, and as his tears flow, he enjoys himself. Does this mean that we love pain? Surely we all want to be happy. Or is it that nobody wants to suffer but does want to feel pity, and as this is not possible without pain, then in this one case pain is enjoyed? This also comes bubbling out of every fount of devoted philanthropism.

But, taking a more serious tone, it says later that through this ardent, theatrical excitement, this devoted feeling flows in *torrentem picis bullientis, aestus immanes tetrarum libidinum etc.*[163]

There is no doubt that Bernays rightly concluded that the "pathos" triggered off in the public has the nature of an ecstasy, an enthusiasm that is objectless, i.e., remaining entirely on the subjective level (see below); in our language we would say "doing without projection." So the immediate effect of sharing in the dramatic events is being moved by God. As we know, Aristotle claimed that this was possible because the spectators felt related (ὁμοῖοι, *homoioi*) to the heroes of the drama. This would be a special form of identification which in turn, applied to the dream, amounts to an understanding "on the subjective level." The famous example that during the performance of "Medea" by Euripides women went into labor and men had screaming fits (Plutarch) tells us clearly at any rate that the Greek public were not cool and snobbish spectators.

After all this, the impression we have is that the Aristotelian catharsis theory of drama, transposed to the dream, raises interesting questions. The dreamer as the sole spectator of his dreams would then have the opportunity to give vent to his complex-like patterns of behavior, to free himself from their cramping effect (anxiety, in Bernays' words). Looked at this way, dreams really would have, as is often claimed, a homeostatic function in themselves.

As mentioned above (Chap. II. 4), the experiments with dream withdrawal seem to confirm this point of view. Dreams cannot simply be dismissed as pure *lusus naturae* and their significance ignored with a "l'art pour l'art" attitude. On the other hand, we would not like to give the impression that we regard this immediate effect of dreams, even those not remembered, as their sole function. We fully agree with the Rabbi Hisda, who said that an uninterpreted dream is like an unread letter.[164] Moreover, there are enough dreams that go beyond this effect, by the very fact, for example, that the dreamer is rudely awakened. In this connection, it is interesting to ascertain whether such a dream follows the dramatic schema, and has a lysis, or whether this cannot be established. Should the latter be the case, then the auxiliary hypothesis suggests itself that the waking itself is the solution. A relatively natural interpretation of this would then be that the problem in question cannot find its solution in the unconscious, but that it is much more the waking conscious that is required, which is why the dreamer must, to a certain extent, be shocked into this state.

These observations all lead us to a further important point in Jungian dream interpretation.

3. Interpretation on the Objective and Subjective Level

Schopenhauer's view of the "ego as the secret theatre director of dreams" contains a maximal moral assertion. The theatre director is responsible for the repertoire and the program, which is not something we would readily agree to with regard to our dreams. But what if this were "secretly" the case? And what if, like Aristotle, we were in a position to imagine the dream figures as "relatives"? Or, to follow Jung's argument, what if the whole thing were a dramatic activating of "our" complexes? If we give serious thought to the *"mea res agitur,"* it would seem to lead to the idea that we are also responsible for our nocturnal performances; which gives an immense moral significance to dreams. The question is, of course, can and may one take it so far?

With regard to this, Schopenhauer's formula needs to be looked at more closely: the ego is defined as the center of consciousness (see Vol. III of this textbook). The dream, on the other hand, is declared to be an eminently unconscious product, so that in terms of modern psychology, Schopenhauer would be contradicting himself. Freud, however, offers evidence that dreams produce mainly "repressed material," with the conscious of course being the repressing authority, i.e., "the secret theatre director." "Secret" here means "indirect," but still primary. We had been hoping to join in St. Augustine's cry of relief when he thanked God for not making him responsible for his dreams, and must now admit that this does not work. The only outlet left to us is the cheap one of computer science which says that dreams are "nothing but junk removal." Anyone who succeeds in clinging to this opinion in the light of "highly structured dreams" should put this book down right now, for he will never be able to become "his own Shakespeare."

Since Freud, the way things have gone with the interpretation of dream figures seems to have been mainly that these figures have been ascribed to or derived from embodied objective people. So it was assumed that if, for example, I dream about my father or my mother, then this related to my personal father, Mr. XY, or my real mother, Mrs. XY, which at first seems to be an obvious conclusion. Jung calls this interpretation on the *objective level*.

But it often happens, to remain with our example, that (a) the Mr. or Mrs. XY in the dream has certain characteristics not shared with the real, objective figures of the actual Mr. or Mrs. XY. Then the dreamer says "It is my father but then again it isn't," or "He is wearing a hat the way my father never did." Or (b) dream figures crop up who, with the best will in the world, cannot be ascribed to people we know, and whose characteristics or actions in the dream we cannot place (one could say "project"), try as we may.

It was incidents like this which led Jung to propose that in such cases we should simply forget trying to interpret on the "objective level," and should look for the corresponding psychic contents within ourselves, which would be interpretation on the *subjective level*. This will of course lead to violent resistance in some cases. One has to imagine that a dream figure can do things or have characteristics that must appear exceedingly objectionable or morally offensive to the conscious attitude or views of the dreamer. To get him to accept the *"tua res agitur"* can be extremely embarrassing if not virtually impossible. But where do dreams come from if not from myself?

In this dilemma not even the pious conviction of the *"somnia a Deo missa"* is of any help; even then, or precisely then, is when confrontation is implacable. If we have flattering dreams we are only too happy to say "j'ai fait ce rêve," but when the reverse is the case, we would rather look for an alibi. We can see then that dream interpretation on the subjective level can hardly be expected to be very popular for it forces us to come to terms with our personality problems, which is not everybody's cup of tea. But it is precisely for this reason that it must be said that it is a genuinely serious psychological approach, which will not tolerate lazy compromise and which makes a clean sweep of the "projection psychology" of a primitive nature.

In practice, however, it is not always easy to distinguish between objective and subjective level interpretations. There are only approximations, thumb rules, for ultimately it will never be possible to say how much or how little any characteristic presented by one of my dream figures coincides with my own system. It takes a *Terence* to be able to say: *Nil humani a me alienum puto.* (Let nothing human be alien to me.) Only too often there will be a feeling of displeasure, and it will often be difficult ensuring that it does not become a feeling of alienation. Opinions will be divided on the question of who is a person to be taken seriously. Projection on the objective level is terribly popular. The "Establishment" will simply have to suffer the unbearable and hence projected dissatisfaction with the situation as it is.

And another, very odd problem presents itself: how is it that half a century after Freud has drawn our attention to the significance of projection, some of the younger generation are tending to project outwards all their internal differences? Many people somatize their psychological problems; today it looks as though they socialize them. Sociology is becoming a playground for projections which should be dealt with on a highly personal level (charity begins at home!), but which are being theoretically butchered on the collective field of sociology with the aid of a load of scientific-sounding jargon. People profess that society can be examined by its own laws, as if it did not consist of individuals, each of whom should be taking his own problems seriously.

According to Jung, the things that can be dealt with on the objective level are:

1. People well-known to the dreamer from his conscious world.
2. Situations well-known to the dreamer from his conscious world.
3. Objective facts with which one has to cope.

All this applies as long as the way they are represented in the dream largely coincides with the objective data. But, as already mentioned above, it will often happen that the father, the boss or the husband appears in the dream and looks, behaves and acts differently from what we experience when awake. In these cases, the characteristics that are different should be looked at on the subjective level, and in this way we see them as the authoritarian, paternal or partner-like principle in ourselves.

Looking at the dream as a whole, the subjective level would then mean that not only is "everybody his own Shakespeare," but even his own Shylock, Antonio, Bassanio, or his own Portia (the latter being in a man his anima; cf. Vol. IV of this textbook). This interpretation is actually contained in principle in Nietzsche's statement: "Nothing is *more* your own than your dream! Nothing is *more* your work! Material, form, duration, actor, spectator—in these comedies you are all yourselves."[165]

4. Compensation[166]

Along with the principle of the subjective level, Jung also attached importance to the idea that in evaluating a dream one should always know the dreamer's conscious, real-life situation. In view of the relation between the two dimensions, he felt he had found a regularity to which there were almost no exceptions. According to his idea, this consisted in a compensatory relationship between dream and consciousness that included the real-life situation. This is where Purkinje may be regarded as Jung's forerunner, for in the work quoted earlier he is always speaking about the compensatory function of dreams. For Jung such a relation exists because of the long stipulated compensatory relationship between conscious and unconscious.

But we need to know more precisely what is to be understood by compensation in psychology. *Compenso* (lat.) means to weigh up against, balance, make up for. Inevitably, this leads to another point of view creeping in insofar as any such balancing has anything functional about it. One might be tempted to say that the unconscious has an "interest" in rectifying any one-sidedness in the conscious situation and that it is putting two points of view side by side for the purpose of balancing or rectifying them.

Theoretically, the difficult question now arises of who it is who actually weighs up these different aspects, or more precisely, who is it who puts forward the point of view of the unconscious to counterbalance the conscious. There is more to this than simple complementation, which would just be an extension (lat. *compleo* = making complete) of something that is missing and could thus very simply be seen purely mechanically as the consequence of the supposed *horror vacui* in Nature. What actually happens is that the compensation presupposes an authority that is informed, that has a higher point of view, which is used not only to give the diagnosis but also the therapy. Moreover, it seems to me theoretically somewhat dissatisfying to see this compensatory effect in just one direc-

An intentionality intending toward wholeness.

tion, namely from the unconscious to the conscious. A symmetrical formula is obviously preferable: unc. ↔ cons.

As is generally known, we find in Jung the concept of the archetype of the self or of wholeness (see later). This term also cannot be dispensed with when dealing with the theory of compensation.

Practical examples of compensatory dream contents usually appear very trivial and are often coarse and crude. For example, a lady who professes to be distinguished can dream about a prostitute or of a woman lying drunk in the gutter. An engineer who is over-rational dreams about his successful construction of a perpetuum mobile of the first order.

It can easily be seen from the above that Jung's theory of compensation opens up a wide field for the cybernetic way of looking at things.

5. *Symbolism*

The symbol plays a central role in Jung's interpretation of the dream. Let us begin by trying to define what a symbol means in Jung. We have to proceed *per exclusionem*, for the expression *symbol* is used with any different number of meanings.

We have already seen that body symbolism has been spoken about in Scherner or Tobia Cohn. Then Silberer talks about threshold symbolism where, for example, departing in the dream stands for the transition from one psychic state (waking) to another (sleeping). The equations set up in all these cases do not contain genuine symbolism in the Jungian sense. What is called a symbol there is an expression for something known (e.g., the lungs, a change in psychic condition and so on). Such a way of describing things is called *semiotic* (Greek σῆμα, *sema* = sign). Such signs are generally analogies or abbreviations designating something that is familiar and concrete. Examples would be the wheel of the Swiss Federal Railways, the benzene ring as the badge of the chemistry student or the rosette in the buttonhole of the chevalier de la légion d'honneur.

A further category of so-called "symbolic" expressions is the *allegory*. This is a deliberate veiling of something familiar or abstract. *Allegorein* (Gk.) means: to say something differently. A modern example is the representation of Justitia as a woman with scales and sword, blindfolded. Or when a charitable organization uses the Christian cross as its badge, it stands metaphorically for Christian charity. The thing about allegories is that with a little thought their meaning can be revealed by analysis.

Jung takes the genuine symbol and compares it with the semiotic expression, analogy and allegory, which are not symbols in the strict sense of the term. His own definition (No. 51) in the book *Psychological Types*[167] is of course unparalleled, but I will nevertheless try to give the main essentials in a few words: the symbol is the best possible description of something that is relatively unknown but for which we have a need. Let us once again take the Christian cross as an example, but this time as a genuine symbol; it is then the expression of a factual situation hitherto unknown and incomprehensible, that is transcendental, and defies all explanation but is most aptly represented by the cross. Insofar as the circumstances concerned are relatively unknown, their symbol is always adapted to even further possibilities in meaning. If, in the course of time, it should come about that this element of unknown is presented in its full extent, then the corresponding symbol would be dead as far as Jung was concerned. It would then have become analogy or allegory. In the symbol, rational and irrational elements are always combined.

It seems to me that we have a classic example of this process in the second vision of Kekulé (cf. Vol. I of this textbook). (Visions may be placed on a par with dreams when it comes to symbolism.) From the history of symbolism we know that the snake ouroboros, the tail-eater, has a wide range of possible meanings. In support of Kekulé it must be stated that at that time the ring structure of the benzene molecule was not only not known but was inconceivable, for the inconsistencies in the known properties of benzene would not allow for this possibility; the reverse is also true that the ancient symbol of the "tail-eater" never allowed for the ring structure of any aromatic compounds. It should be clear that in the form of the ouroboros we have all the defining elements of the genuine symbol. It appears spontaneously here, from an unmistakably unconscious background, and gives Kekulé a shock (emotion) and gives new impulse to his thinking and puts him on a new track.

Let us recall here the function of the trident in the first dream of our patient (p. 8), which also fits in with the definition of the genuine symbol (as does the fish, by the way). And this also had a dramatic effect in the process of medical history. Kekulé's struggle with the benzene problem actually found its lysis with this symbol (*deus ex machina*). And only then came the creative thinking that led to the intellectual mastering of the problem of the hitherto inexplicable concrete properties of benzene. For Kekulé the ouroboros had then fulfilled its purpose as a symbol and since then the benzene ring is no longer a symbol, being dead as such, but still serves as a sema for the affiliations of the chemistry student. But the fact that Kekulé did not forget the "Symbols in Action," but thought of them with awe, as still emerges so clearly from his jubilee speech 25 years later (Vol. I of this textbook), speaks for the fact that he was a man of great culture, both on the human and the spiritual levels.

Perhaps we should get certain facts straight at this point: all too often we hear about the creative quality of the unconscious. I regard this as misleading. True, the unconscious produces symbols like the above. But it is *also* a misapplication to describe Nature as creative, for although it is productive, it is never anything completely new (the mutations may be an exception here). The same applies to symbols, for basically they are all known. Granted, no two trees are alike, but we do not regard each one as a new creation. In the same way symbols are always individual insofar as their variants depend on the individual history of their bearer, but the essence of each has long been known. So the creative aspect of the unconscious takes place at best only in its fruitful confrontation with the conscious.

It might be useful here to look more closely at the etymology of the word symbol. συμβάλλω (*symballo*) means to join together, to unite two (or more) separate units: σύμβολον (*symbolon*) is each half of an object which together form a whole. The best-known example is the fragments of a clay vessel in ancient times which the guest receives and the host keeps. By means of the two fragments that fit together, both men can identify each other as friends at any time. This was the origin of the *tessera hospitalis* of the Romans, which was a mark of recognition. As such it is also a sign or emblem. In the mysteries it has the meaning of the password, as can be seen in Plutarch, for example, in the *consolatio ad uxorem* 10: τὰ μυστικὰ σύμβολα τῶν περὶ τὸν Διόνυσον ὀργιασμῶν (And through the mystic symbol of the Dionysian rite), to which Cicero referred (Tuscul. I, 29): *reminiscere, quoniam es initiatus, quae tradantur mysteriis* (and remember what has been handed down in the mysteries, as you belong to the initiated). This is where the further meaning of the term *symbolon* comes in, namely that of omen, containing the idea of *knowing* more than what is actually known and can be experienced.

In 1937 I had a Dutch experimental psychologist (47 years old) in training analysis. As the dream analysis progressed he started to experience small visions. They became more and more coherent (think of Silberer's lecanomantic viewing) and as they did so they gained in significance. It is not possible here to describe these developments, but I should like to put up for discussion one of these images, which turned out to be more or less definitive:

> A central, red, transparent sphere, which I call the "inside one," is rotating on its lateral axis from front to back. Around it there is a large, blue outside sphere. This is rotating in a clockwise direction, more rapidly than the "inside" sphere. In the "inside" sphere there is a "luminous cross." It is lying horizontally in the equator of the sphere and is right-angled. Its arms are "tubes of light," in which the "light" is pumped rhythmically from the center to the periphery. As it reaches the periphery, this rhythmically flowing light dissolves into clouds of red lustre. To the left of this there stands a female figure who, with outstretched arm, points imperiously to the whole scene.

This vision can really only be understood as a symbol. It is a purely formal-dynamic schema, which has a very abstract effect, but the only human element, the woman, explicitly points to its significance. This woman, however, is completely impersonal and not reducible to the objective. So she belongs on the subjective level. She has to be understood as Mystagogue (anima, see later). Looked at from the formal point of view, the image is a typical dynamic mandala, known to us from numerous publications of Jung's, i.e., a representative of the psycho-physical totality of Man. That is why we find in it unambiguous references to bodily functions (see body "symbolism" earlier) such as the pulse. The pulsating of the light (cf. the "circulation of light" in Taoism or the Dharma Wheel in Buddhism)[168] is brought by the analysand into relation with his own rhythm, which he had always felt to be too quick and which had been "tamed" in many earlier dreams. In the vision, the "light pulse" now has a subjectively satisfying and comforting frequency. One could call this heart symbolism, but in the psycho-physical sense, not in the anatomical-physiological sense, i.e., the heart as the seat of feeling if not of the soul, or as the center of this psycho-physical totality.

There is a clear case of color symbolism in the two spheres (red and blue), which according to tradition would express the opposing pair of feeling and thinking. (Actually we could dwell at length here on psychological typology, but this is not the place.) And anyway, red appears again for the light impulses dissolve into red clouds.

What is particularly striking is the symbolism of form, for we have here what is esentially a geometrical structure: spheres, coordinate system of axes, center. We know from Jung that such forms always express wholeness, totality.

Emphasis must be given to the dynamic symbolism: two moments of rotation and a rhythmic impulse, all with different time functions (frequency).

It is an insuperable problem that hermeneutics (= doctrine of the activity of Hermes!), which gets to the root of such problems, comes up against too many difficulties. The very fact that we would have to know the whole life story of the subject fairly well if we are to give adequate consideration to the personal aspects of a symbol means that a satisfactory representation is virtually impossible, for it would take several volumes. The same applies to the compensatory function of the unconscious product, as it does anyway to the very important consideration of the conscious, real situation *and* unconscious. The rational elements would have to be dealt with, but what about the irrational ones! We must also realize that present, past and future are contained in the factor t of our case, which manifests itself so clearly in the different speeds of rotation of the two spheres or in the pulsations.

In view of all these differences, we content ourselves with saying that it is a mandala, a symbol of the self, which, in accordance with its "transcendental function" is able to unite opposites. But this cannot be dealt with till we come to the fourth volume of this textbook. Furthermore, Jung has commented at length on these terms in several passages.

It is not exactly common for such symbols to form with this simplicity and clarity. But, as we have already stated, the symbols are well-known and found everywhere. An unusual example of this is the fact that in 1938 Jung gave the Terry Lectures at Yale and referred to a case in which a vision occurred which bears a striking resemblance to the one described above. It is the vision of the "world-clock" in *Psychology and Religion*.[169] That patient was being treated neither by Jung nor by myself, and in 1937 I knew nothing about the material Jung was working on for Yale. So there is no question of any collusion on the part of the two subjects. They were total strangers and from different racial and cultural backgrounds; my student was a psychologist, and Jung's subject was a physicist. Is this sufficient evidence of the ubiquitousness of symbols? Or should one put in a word for Jung's hypothesis of synchronicity to understand this amazing coincidence?

6. Typical Motifs

As mentioned in the introduction, we have today at our disposal a method (Hall and Van de Castle) of making a statistical survey of specific dream elements. The appearance of symbols and their correlates is urgently in need of such a system. This is especially true for typical dream motifs, for many of them have a habit of appearing in certain sequences. But even without this statistical material, we can say on the basis of experience that dreams with similar motifs group themselves round a definite problem in any given period of time, a problem which is just coming to the surface (being constellated). If we arrange these dreams graphically round the center of meaning, we get a similar schema to that for amplification (p. 14). Judging from this, it looks as though the *dreams themselves procure the amplification method*, and would persistently circle the problem center until enough light has been thrown on it.

It is precisely with regard to this question that the statistical method would be particularly useful. We have long known what are typical motifs, and one has only to think of Silberer (threshold symbolism). Among them are departure, transition, crossing a stretch of water—e.g., by swimming, by boat, over a ford or bridge—falling, flying, caves and their dangers, jewels and dragons, animals in general, both rapacious and helpful ones, especially snakes, circumambulation and nocturnal sea voyages. With the last-mentioned, one thinks of Jonah, to whose myth Leo Frobenius[170] collected primitive parallels, thus inaugurating comparative motif research. Any exhaustive dealings with the unconscious corresponds in its procedure to this common denominator, with its dangers and peripetiea. Motif research has achieved great results in fairy tales and myths and produced many hitherto unsuspected insights (cf. Bolte and Polivka[171]). It is essentially a comparative method in which it is necessary to bear in mind the prerequisites and connections of cultural history, for they make an important contribution to the understanding of the function of myths.

Now comes a series of features which seem to be more or less characteristic of the dream impression.

7. Contamination

Contamination comes from the Latin *contaminare* = to make impure. Discrimination being the prerogative of the conscious, it is of course absent in the unconscious sphere. Accordingly, it can be stated that the contents of the unconscious have no clear outlines, cannot easily be separated, and overlap on all sides, and so on. This state creates the impression that everything is related to everything else (H. von Hofmannsthal, Ariadne auf Naxos: "Nothing is pure here, everything came to everything else.")

The term is a product of extreme conceptualization of which only the conscious is capable. But in the unconscious we have *pars pro toto*, which takes us into the actual sphere of "free association," which, as Freud has shown, is anything but free, precisely for this reason. Contamination is particularly striking when it crops up in the conscious sphere, namely as the effect of a complex; under it our ability to make distinctions diminishes greatly in clarity. So anyone with an activitated jealousy complex is reminded of Othello by just any old handkerchief. Another example of contamination is when Jung's patient said: "I am the Lorelei," because the doctors replied to to her double Dutch by saying "Ich weiss nicht was soll es bedeuten" ("I don't know what this means")—the opening line of the famous Lorelei song by Heine. The same patient declared herself to be a "Socrates subtitute" because, like Socrates, she felt she was being kept in the clinic unfairly.[172] Dreams or dream elements frequently have this feature of contaminiation, which often makes them seem incoherent and difficult to unravel.

8. *Condensation*

Condensation cannot really be separated from contamination. It happens when a dream content can combine the characteristics of several contents which are kept separate in the conscious. We have seen an example of this in the crab-saurian in the dream mentioned by Jung (p. 88, first example by Jung), where it is a chimera, familiar to us from the figure decorations of Gothic cathedrals or illuminated Irish manuscripts, and which remind us of biology. The commonest are dream figures which are made up, or are a blend of qualities of totally different acquaintances. This is true of the case I have already mentioned where I appeared in my patient's dreams endowed with the qualities of his dentist.

9. *Multiplication*

Multiplication is the opposite of condensation in that it multiplies a single dream element. One could think that it is a particular emphasis of the element concerned, on the lines of "you must say it three times" (Faust). But if the motif is just doubled, we must not forget the well-known fact that one can have double vision, if one is drunk, for example. Then the two retina images cannot be merged, which obviously demands a certain conscious effort that naturally cannot be fully made in sleep. But not all dream elements are in duplicate, so this interpretation is not generally satisfactory. It seems rather that the double vision is a sort of reflection effect which appears with objects which are situated roughly on the horizon line conscious/unconscious, i.e., appearing in both spheres.

I recall dream V of the Zeeman effect in my incubation study.[173] It runs as follows:

> An unknown woman brings me plums for dessert and at the same time a man's voice in the background says: "You must eat this fruit in order to be able to do the experiment with the Zeeman effect."

The Zeeman effect consists of the magnetic splitting of a spectrum line into three lines (with the undisturbed original line in the middle) or into several lines. The dream reminds us of a passage in "The Secret of the Golden Flower," a Chinese meditation text,[174] where it says: "The sun sinks in the large water and magic images of rows of trees appear." As it says later in the text, it is a "Sevenfold row of trees." So in this meditation, when the light of consciousness (sun) touches the surface of the water (horizon consc./unconsc.) or in the "pole-free state" Wu Gi of the text, there comes into being a sevenfold image, which gives us a classical example of multiplication. Unfortunately, we are a long way from really understanding this remarkable phenomenon of multiplication, which is all the more regrettable in that it is of such great interest.

10. Concretization

Another well-known feature of dreams is that they seem to like turning certain characteristics of the dream figures into concrete images. For example, a black dog in a dream can stand for the dreamer's "bête noire" or for "des Pudels Kern" (the gist of the matter). If such expressions are to be understood, obviously one has to be familiar with the figures of speech, as is the case with "body symbolism." Complexes are personified in the dream, and they can of course be represented by animals if they are "animal" enough. In practice, the tendency to create conscious images is carried to great extremes and leads to the fact that in dreams we get to hear "little stories" instead of simple facts, which can easily turn the dream into a literal chinoiserie. In fact, the Chinese seem to have a similar "mentality," which is why Jung used to say jokingly that if we ask a Chinese to bring a blade of grass he will roll up with a whole meadow.

11. Dramatization

Acting and dramatizing is a tendency of primitive man, and hence of the primitive man in us, which comes to the fore in the products of our unconscious. We are not talking here about the dramatic structure of the dream, which we have already discussed and to which we shall return later, but about the simple fact that in dreams a psychic situation is not usually represented as such, in the juristic-abstract sense, but by means of actions and procedures, from which we then have to derive or deduce the content represented. Complete lengthy ceremonies, such as the "Morgestraich" of a Basle carnival, are experienced instead of a brief reference to the example to the effect that evil spirits are being exorcized.

12. Archaization

The tendency towards archaization lies along the same lines as the primitive tendencies. The term may be a pleonasm, for the unconscious is itself archaic. Essentially it is historic, even prehistoric and primitive, which is why it happens the way it does in dreams (the assigned tasks of earlier generations with Nietzsche). Looked at like this, it is no surprise when animals speak, i.e., when our "bush soul" stirs, or when all sorts of magic acts and effects take place.

13. Suggestions on How To Process Dream Material in a Useful Way

The following remarks are to be seen as an attempt to put forward reasonably systematic approaches to the processing of dream material. There are two things we are *not* aiming at: (1) Providing a universally valid "key" for dream interpretation, and (2) achieving completeness, which would contradict our opening remarks that the individual dream should only be approached with the greatest possible openness.

What we *are* striving for are answers to two other questions:
1. What method of questioning is appropriate to the dream and how can it best be done?

2. How can we capture the essence of the dream, exclusively from the point of view of its individual way of functioning? In this way we will learn to understand better what the dream has to say about the functioning of the unconscious psyche when it is allowed to develop in an unadulterated way. What we basically intend to do is to adhere to the phenomenonological aspect of the dream and under no circumstances come up with a "recipe for dream analysis."

If the fisherman dreams about fishing (*piscator pisces somniat*), this fact (which has yet to be proved!) is not to be understood causally as an echo of what preoccupies him consciously but as the special way, under the pretext of his job, in which the fisherman's unconscious psyche best speaks to him, this being the way most suited to his psyche. As we have stated, what we aim to learn from all our efforts is how the unconscious is constituted in form and function. So our point of view is scientific and not "applied," i.e., therapeutic. A somewhat therapeutic side product would nevertheless lie in the fact that such a closer understanding of the dynamic of the unconscious would enable one to see oneself and one's fellowmen more impartially. An effect that is certainly not to be despised.

So, first of all, we are going to think about what principles we actually have at our disposal when it comes to scientifically approaching a dream. In so doing we shall basically stick to Jung's notes "Zur Methodik der Traumdeutung"[175] which he used for his dream seminars at the E.T.H.

These considerations are all based on the conclusion that the dream is a natural psychic phenomenon that cannot be produced by a conscious act of will. Indirectly this means that the dream is a product of the unconscious psyche, a conclusion that is anything but trivial for there are constant disputes as to whether such a statement is meaningful. We do not wish to burden ourselves or the reader with these arguments, which mainly come from philosophical quarters. Any doctor with psychiatric experience can see clearly from comparative considerations with psychopathological material what is meant by the statement above and the difference from the conscious act of will is obvious to him.

Moreover, it would not only be futile but actually wrong to draw conclusions from dream statements in the hope of expanding the conscious if these dream statements did not enjoy a great deal of "Fool's privilege" with regard to the conscious. We would then only learn what we already know, and the unconscious would be nothing more than the "sediment" of the conscious. Evidence that this is not the case lies in the fact that no living man has ever succeeded in definitively decanting the conscious from the unconscious psyche; what is more, we experience only too frequently how very different we can be in our dreams from what we think we are, and how often, when we give it honest consideration, these surprises, once we have overcome our resistance to them, have to be acknowledged as true, precisely in those areas where we had not consciously expected it. And the fact that the dream makes use of our conscious language and images from our conscious world of sense perception is no argument against the dream as a psychic phenomenon. It is the very fact that the dream has the resources of consciousness at its disposal that makes it communicate at all.

But we do know that the unconscious can be different from the conscious and this was made very clear by the elementary phenomena presented in Vol. I of this textbook. And it is precisely because the unconscious and the dream can also be very different from the contents of the conscious that since time immemorial Man has felt obliged to interpret these signs. Thus one would like to explain what cannot be and what has not been understood, which raises the big question of what possibilities are open to us for going about this.

We have seen that there is no known experimental set-up capable of producing a definite dream to order. The most one can do is to make it probable that specific isolated impulses recur in the dream, but in a most unspecific manner, totally altered, and just as elements. So it would be better to forgo applying any causal form of explanation. Jung recommends a "conditionalistic" approach. What he means is that one should take into account all the conditions under which the specific phenomenon of this dream came about. But when it comes to following and understanding the course of a dream, we can never make deductions from the causal thought scheme. What actually happens is that we are obliged to look at every step of the action as the result of the previous step i.e., stipulate a causal process between the individual events, otherwise we would have to abandon any hope of understanding from the word go. This principle is always valid, even when there is no apparent logical connection or when the process seems absurd and totally incoherent.

We now attempt to establish what recognizable sources the dream has at its disposal.

(a) It seems obvious that contents of the conscious can appear in our dreams, e.g., impressions from the previous day and conscious preoccupations. As we know, Freud calls them "remnants of the day." They are "remnants" in that they are still lying around on the stage, like forgotten props that are still lying around on the stage, like forgotten props that are now used ad hoc for the improvised nocturnal performance. But we should like to point out here that such elements are hardly ever found in the dream *tale quale*. Whether it is something one has thought or experienced, living or dead objects, a thorough examination of the details will invariably reveal that they have altered slightly in one way or another. We cannot blame these variations on the "imprecision of dream language" for in many other respects the dream usually has an extremely precise form of expression. What is more, in practice it turns out to be well worthwhile looking at these very differences carefully, for they often make us aware of matters which had escaped our waking observation. From this some people have concluded that our unconscious perception (subliminal perception) is considerably more accurate than our conscious one, an idea that is difficult to prove but cannot be lightly dismissed.

(b) Most dream contents, however, will defy this derivation from the conscious so we are forced to assume that their origins lie in the unconscious. We also assume that these are not just any contents but those necessary to "manufacture" the particular dream. This is what we call the constellated content of the unconscious. What this means is that it is precisely these and no others which, having been prompted at the time, are to a certain extent ionized. They would distinguish themselves from (a) in that they were not once contents of the conscious, i.e., not simply forgotten or repressed. Thus dream sources can fall into two main categories: (1) constellations occasioned indirectly by conscious contents, and (2) constellations occasioned directly by unconscious processes.

The second category, as we see, already corresponds to an autonomous activity on the part of the unconscious, in no recognizable way dependent on the conscious. The many findings discussed in the first volume of this textbook confirm that this is not mere speculation. This category entails far-reaching conclusions as regards the autonomousness of the unconscious, imbuing dreams with a totally independent function in that it is perfectly feasible for the unconscious to be of a different opinion from the conscious.

This concludes what we know about the possible *roots* of dreams; we shall now follow the same principles in looking at the possible *functions* of dreams.

As we stated earlier, there are, in connection with the "new biology of dreaming," a whole series of hypotheses on the function of the dream, but they all confine themselves to the physiological sphere, as if the dream were only a physical phenomenon. It is of course this as well, being linked with metabolic processes of its substratum, the brain. So there is no denying its right to exist from a "mental-mechanical" point of view. If anyone with an engineering mentality sees the dream as the "junk removal" of the computer's brain, this may well be a fascinating concept but does not allow the dream any psychological function at all in the strictest sense of the term. Such an attitude ignores the psychic aspect altogether, or even denies it. As this negation is in itself a psychic act, the whole thing gets taken to ridiculous extremes.

The idea of this minor digression is to emphasize that in this section we wish to deal exclusively with the *purely psychological interpretation of the dream*. We consider it right and necessary to try to understand a psychic product within its own milieu, i.e., the psychological one. There can of course be many psychological functions. One of them should be the "meaning," and it is precisely the meaning of the dream that has led since time immemorial to so many methods of interpretation.

Whether this meaning is something that we bring in *a posteriori* or whether, being inherent in the dream, it has to be discovered by us first, is a paradoxical problem of epistemology. But the meaning of my dream is related to me as the dreamer, and as it is or will be meaningful to me alone, I have gained an asset, learned something, which in turn is only possible as a result of the dream transcending the conscious. After the age of "enlightenment" has only just really begun, the idea of the dream being a genuine psychic phenomenon, to be taken seriously, is in jeopardy of being damned as "superstition." The psychologist, who is convinced of the outstanding reality of the psyche in his day-to-day practical experience with people, cannot share this basically materialistic idea. Nor will he on the other hand be able to deny the justification of chemistry and physics or anatomy and physiology. Not everyone who looks at the moon lapses into space fantasies; no more do the dogs who bark at it. But what they experience is for them immeasurably more important than a piece of moon rock, because its effects are felt immediately. Now one can in these cases, too, try to examine these effects more closely and perhaps try to understand them, so that one then has grasped more of the microcosm.

The interpretation of meaning has always been one of the most distinguished philosophical and religious mainsprings, but the expression does not have much appeal for scientific tastes. Whether the idea of the dream as "brain urine" has more appeal is a matter of opinion. We shall try to do justice to the different attitudes by looking at the word "interpretation" in its Latin sense; *interpretatio* does not just have the general Ciceronian meaning of the explanation *ostentorum et somniorum*, but also the special meaning of the elucidation of an expression by the one following it, an approach which goes well with the amplification process discussed earlier.

When inquiring into the possible meaning, purpose or function of the dream, it is opportune to take as a starting point its position in relation to the situation of the dreamer's consciousness. In this respect we can distinguish four different possibilities:

1. The dream represents the unconscious reaction to the conscious situation. It can often be shown that the dream adds an aspect to the conscious situation that had escaped us. Usually it is a case of habitual onesidedness in our attitude toward something we have perceived or experienced, which in this way is completed by what the dream depicts. So it is a complement through something that is objectively missing, but a *condition* of this is the impression of the day. It is different and more complicated when we are dealing with compensation (see above), which takes us to the second possibility.

2. The dream represents a situation that has arisen from the conflicts between conscious and unconscious. A *prerequisite* for such a possibility is the independence of the unconscious. Thus this second stage involves a further step in the direction of the autonomy of the unconscious.

3. The dream represents a tendency of the unconscious which is aimed at changing the conscious attitude. In such cases it must be assumed that the *potential of the unconscious* is greater than that of the conscious, thus making its autonomy maximal. This is why these are always highly emotional, significant-seeming dreams, which are actually in a position to bring about a change in the conscious or, as we usually say, a change of mind.

4. Finally there are dreams which represent unconscious processes which do not seem to have any connection with the conscious. They are usually regarded as "big dreams" and often have the character of illumination or even of an oracle. This category certainly includes those dreams which with Macrobius, for example, are called *somnia a Deo missa*. The stimuli necessary for such dreams to come

about vary widely, so that there is something non-uniform about this class. This means that it is necessary to make a further subdivision according to the type of "stimulus":

First, there are processes in the *somatic* sphere. The correlation psyche/soma is exceptionally high, on the one hand (think of voluntary movements, for example), but also very weak on the other (intellectual freedom). At any rate, there are no precise laws in this sphere. As always in such cases, the correlation can be seen most frequently in the sphere of pathology, i.e., in extreme cases. This is probably why doctors such as Hippocrates and Galen taught their students how to read dreams as if they were symptoms and thus became able to make use of them both diagnostically and prognostically. But the correlation is a weak one, and because of that their arguments are extremely difficult to follow. What it probably was in actual fact in the individual cases was a combination of clinical observation and experience together with medical-psychological intuition. And anyway there cannot be a reliable therapy without the somatic data. After this warning it seems fitting to quote a case where although I did not make the diagnosis from the dream, the clinical report afterwards confirmed the dream diagnosis:

The dream subject was an apparently perfectly healthy middle-aged man, who had the following dream on December 24, 1948: "Looking in the mirror I see that there is a silver thread coming out of my right temple and I start to pull it out with a pair of tweezers. At first I have to proceed very carefully and I have the impression that the thread is very long."

In the second dream the same man noted "that my right temple was 'cured,' i.e., the skin looked like parchment as if it had dried up after a wound."

In mid-April 1949 the dreamer developed neurological symptoms indicating the presence of a tumor with the ensuing space-consuming pressure inside the skull. At the exact point indicated in the dream it was possible to diagnose an extradural meningioma, which was removed by operation on May 10th. It had the silvery color of the thread in the dream and measured $7 \times 5 \times 4$ cm. The patient has been in good health ever since.

In connection with this we recall a special complication that can never be ruled out and likewise can only be recognized *ex eventu*: somatic sources of disturbance can be due to psychic processes, although we are not thinking first and foremost here of so-called psychosomatic medicine. It is our opinion that autonomous, purely psychical processes in the unconscious sometimes cannot find any, or any adequate, psychological expression, either in dreams or by stimulating the conscious; there are processes which (to use an awful word of my own coinage) are not, nor not yet, "psychifiable." It is particularly these that lead to somatic manifestations and in this roundabout way can occasion dreams of this first category. The roundabout route we have just described is nothing more than a special model for the famous but largely not understood psychophysical relation, which should here be read in both directions. Disturbances of this kind are usually of a functional nature, but take place in the bodily sphere, so that we unhesitatingly allocate them to somatic sources, even where they have grown primarily on psychic soil. This is excusable, if only for the fact that we are now in the sphere where the psyche becomes physical and the physical psychic, i.e., where the dividing line becomes blurred.

Second, there are dream sources that are the consequence of physical occurrences in the immediate environment, such as noises or experimentally set-up impulses as used in laboratories today, or those used by Mourly Vold for example. The still topical famous dream of Maury (see above) also belongs in this class.

Third, there are purely psychic occurrences in the environment which can express themselves in dreams, a fact which takes some understanding, especially when the psychic processes are going on in people the dreamer could not know anything about.

It will be recognized at once that we are now in the sphere of parapsychology, although before any conclusions are reached careful checks must always be made as to whether the phenomenon cannot be explained with the aid of subliminal perceptions, in which case no "extrasensory channel" need be called on. Jung describes such a case which in our opinion can hardly be sorted out without the hypothesis of telepathy: "A child dreams that his mother is killing herself, wakes up in terror and runs into the mother's bedroom to find that she is in fact about to commit suicide."

Another example from my own experience—a schoolboy's dream—runs as follows: "I am in the X mental hospital, apparently as a patient. I am with another patient in a groundfloor room. In front of the open window I see a large basket hanging on a rope which is going up. I assume that from an upper floor a child has let the basket down. I pick up a teddy bear which is lying in the room to put it in the basket. As I get to the window, there are two men standing outside, one of whom fires a shot at me with a pistol. I immediately run away from the window, wondering whether I have been hit, which doesn't seem to be the case."

The schoolboy is awakened by this dream or by the telephone, which is just ringing. He is informed by the same mental hospital X that his uncle, who was in the hospital because of depression, had just died totally unexpectedly. Let us recall at this point what we said earlier about the spherical shape (pistol bullet).

Two more possible dream sources now come under discussion and in both of them the factor t (time) seems to play an unusual role.

There are dream contents deriving from past events in the environment. These are, of course, as trivial as Freud's "remnants of the day." But the problem becomes difficult when such elements relate to the past but were probably never contents of the conscious. It might be very difficult in the individual case to ascertain this last-mentioned condition beyond all doubt, for in the course of time we have seen, heard, read and completely forgotten such a tremendous amount. But there are experiences which allow us to conclude that none of this vast material is ever really lost, so that in many cases of this kind a possible explanation would be a cryptomnesia (see Vol. I of this textbook), which would mean that such a dream motif does not belong in this category.

But Jung thinks that occasionally historical names or objects, for example, crop up in dreams and that the dreamer has no conscious knowledge of them. Maybe they are the names of saints, whose legends are genuinely unknown to the dreamer. If one takes the trouble to read the lives of these saints, one can ascertain to one's amazement that a very typical characteristic of a given saint's life corresponds exactly to the dreamer's situation. As one can see, this is a special form of amplification that involves bringing in objective comparison material, in this case of a historical or mythological nature. The conclusion therefore is *ex effectu* that in such a case it is archetypal material or an archetypal situation, i.e., a situation to which the unconscious has always reacted with a more or less typical visual concept, even at the time when the myth or legend was created.

But if the unconscious is supposed to have genuinely produced these names or legends—i.e., before they were consciously absorbed—then it remains a complete mystery how the unconscious could have come to this knowledge, and the only conceivable answer is the bold hypothesis of its "omniscience." Jung himself would put in a plea for this possibility, having become keenly aware of such things through his vast experience with archetypical material, which led him to far-reaching arguments based on analogy. I doubt whether the other hypothesis of the reversal of the sense of time (t-factor) is of much use here.

As a fifth and final possibility for showing that unconscious processes can affect dreams without ever having had any connection with the conscious, there is that one that reveals that future events in the environment can trigger off dreams. It is perfectly clear that this is a purely parapsychological phenomenon, for what we have here is precognition. In popular belief (or superstititon, as some might prefer to call it), we hear a lot about "foreboding" or "prophecy," and in German there is a saying that major events cast their shadows ahead of them. A number of psychoanalysts with parapsychological leanings have taken the trouble to collect such cases, which are by no means as rare as one tends to assume.[176] We have already given one example and will give another one here, taken from Jung's own experience.

A patient, a middle-aged woman, suddenly had the following alarming dream in the middle of a series of ordinary dreams: "She was alone in a house. It was evening and she went to close the windows. It occurred to her that there was a back door to be closed, but it had no lock so she decided to barricade it with furniture. It grew darker and more eery. Suddenly the door burst open and a dark ball forced its way into the room and drove straight into her body."

The background-context of the dream is as follows: it is the house of an aunt in the USA. The dreamer had last been there twenty years earlier. Since then the family had broken up because of serious differences, and in particular there had been no contact between the dreamer and this aunt for twenty years. Jung wrote to the dreamer's sister asking for information, and the facts given by the dreamer were fully confirmed (objective anamnesis, see below).

A few days after the above dream, the dreamer had a letter from America saying that her aunt had died on the day of the dream.

One step further in this direction is taken by dreams that are precognitive in the strictest sense of the term, i.e., those that depict a situation which, understood as a real-life situation, actually only happened in the distant or not too distant future, and largely or completely without any intervention on our part. Anyone who does not keep a detailed record of his dreams (remember Synesius' "Night Journal")—i.e., does not always write them down at once, and give the exact date—will hardly be able to perceive such events, let alone prove they happened. But when we have the opportunity to observe lengthy dream series where such safety measures have been taken, as can happen in analysis, it is striking that precognitive dreams are far from rare. Nor do they only occur with people one would expect to have any particular talent for parapsychology. The parapsychologists have concluded that the factor Ψ (parapsychological ability) is in everyone and that it belongs to the unconscious psyche, which is something of a platitude.

In both theory and practice such occurrences are a problem. Theoretically, because the factor t (time) is wrong, and in practice because at the moment we can't understand such dreams. When one has "interpreted" such a dream *lege artis*, then when the concrete event actually happens, one has the opportunity to smile knowingly about oneself and one's talent. These dreams can only be "explained" *ex eventu*, if explanation is the right word. This abnormality becomes rather sinister when the future event takes on the nature of a catastrophe, be it large or small, and when there is no recognizable personal connection between the catastrophe and the dreamer. One really has to ask the question of why this particular person was selected or burdened with this announcement. At any rate, the naive question about what it all means is no longer adequate here. For even if one were in a position to recognize the connection with a real-life event in the future, which seems quite impossible, one would be totally unable to do anything about it properly, i.e., play Providence.

The famous aerodynamics engineer J. W. Dunne[177] who was, among other things, involved in the development of the Handley-Page wing, and hence can be regarded as a reliable observer, wrote a book called *An Experiment with Time*, in which he describes a number of impressive experiments of this kind, based on his own experience. This problem of time prompted him to write a second book, *The Serial Universe*,[178] in which he develops an ingenious theory in an attempt to explain the apparent inversion of time. None of his explanations, however, can be said to be convincing.

This brings us to the end of our observations on possible dream sources. Jung himself has a few more general points to make:

1. The dream is never a simple photographically faithful reproduction of past events. Jung makes an exception to this rule for the so-called shock dreams which could be observed, for example, with shell shock after the First World War; these dreams used to recur regularly for years, in identical form, and it was always an exact reproduction of the original pathogenic experience, e.g., being buried in the trenches. Traumata have the characteristic of becoming fixed, like "imprints," and do not lend themselves easily to being "psyched out" (an aspect which must also be taken into consideration for the so-called traumata or compensation neuroses).

We have already mentioned variations that the real-life experience undergoes in the dream. Even when the difference is slight, the question is still justified as to why the unconscious takes this extra trouble, especially when this slight difference tells us something that we would otherwise have missed, and it seems more economical to reproduce what had been seen or experienced *tale quale*.

2. The dream brings out unconscious contents which either a) have lost their original link with the conscious, or b) never had such a link. In the case of 2(a), it may be something we have forgotten, but recalling what we said in Volume I, we must bear in mind that there are at least two ways of forgetting something: first the normal, as it were, based simply on the fact that the information we have forgotten is totally devoid of interest for us; second, there is the forgetting which is the effect of a complex, which can then be understood as repression in the Freudian sense.

Compared with this, possibility 2(b) seems to be more difficult to accept for it presupposes that the unconscious has a life of its own, has its own processes and development and follows its own laws. As we have already intimated several times, it is then possible that these processes are not even capable of becoming conscious, or at any rate are not conscious yet. This leads to conclusions which are of significance for dream psychology: the alien nature of certain dreams or dream elements and motifs, and the fact that usually we do not understand our dreams, and so on.

If we go along with Jung in the view that the dream describes our own inner situation, that it is a sort of monologue or inner dialogue (ψυχὴ μόνον πρὸς μόνον, *psyche monou pros monon*, Plotinus), then it is disappointing if not actually nonsensical for us not to understand it. But it is precisely this fact that should teach us to understand how different the unconscious is from the conscious. It is in our own interests never to cease to be amazed at this, i.e., to have as few preconceived theories as possible about what the unconscious is, and to accept its autonomy, with all its questionable aspects as well as its unsuspected possibilities, and to bear in mind that it is by no means certain that we are so much in touch with ourselves.

3. It can happen that the dream presents future contents of the personality which are not and cannot be recognized as such in the present. This represents an extension of point 2(b), but the unconscious contents which have never had a connection with the conscious are given a special rank when it comes to personality development.

This concept motivated Jung with his special concern, childhood dreams. This is not the place to report on the childhood dream seminars which he held at the E.T.H. All we can do is repeat the basic problem: is it not the case that the individual pattern of personality development already exists very early on, and under certain circumstances can be recognized? If that is the case, then it would be possible that the pattern begins to emerge or disclose itself in childhood dreams. As experience with mature or maturing people has shown that the intended wholeness of the personality has the tendency to manifest itself in mandala-like images, it is natural to expect such structures in childhood dreams with their individual variations. Judging from the results of the seminar, it can be claimed that they seem to confirm the hypothesis.

It cannot be denied that this throws light on an idea which otherwise strikes us as rather odd, namely, the idea of dreams as prophecies. Of course, the argument is put forward that dreams come from God, or that in dreams we are particularly "open" to "pneuma" influences from the cosmos, with which we are in such close contact, in accordance with the macro-microcosmos equation. But are these theories so different from ours, especially from Jung's last suggestion that it is possible for future "components" of the personality to reveal themselves in dreams? In this connection one should recall Jung's inaugural dissertation,[179] in which he describes a case where a symbol of wholeness (not yet recognized as a mandala) appears even in youth, and only the later history confirmed the completion of the personality. But if the individuation process described by Jung is more than a rare work of art, which we are firmly convinced is the case, then it must correspond to a design that is always there somewhere, and which makes its presence felt in certain phases of life.

CHAPTER V

THE TECHNIQUE OF RESOLVING THE
MEANING OF DREAMS

"I will get Peter Quince to
write a ballad of this dream.
It shall be call'd 'Bottom's
Dream,' because it hath no
bottom;
—Shakespeare,
A Midsummer Night's Dream
Act IV. Sc.i 220–22

How it comes about that we have to resolve our dreams in order
to understand them is an obvious question, but nonetheless a
difficult one. As we have demonstrated, in the dream we are talking to ourselves (subjective level), or we are looking at a film that
we ourselves are making. And yet we still do not understand ourselves, or only with great difficulty.

In the Talmud, of course, it says that the dream is its own interpreter, but this does not really sink in with us. Still, I must recall
experiences which have constantly surprised me: occasionally there
have appeared in my consulting room people of very old cultures—
Sephardic Jews, Arabs, Ethiopians. When I asked them about their
dreams and then naively set about making tentative comments on
them, I was soon put in my place: these people took it for granted
that they understood their own dreams; in other words they were
still "on speaking terms" with their unconscious.

118

In the *Midrasch Hagadol* there is a very clear passage on the subject and I should like to reproduce Ginzberg's[180] quotation. It refers to Joseph's interpretation of Pharaoh's dreams (Gen. 41.25ff.): "Joseph asked the King first whence he knew that the interpretation given by the wise men of his country was not true, and the Pharaoh replied: 'I saw the *dream and its interpretation together* and therefore they cannot make a fool of me.' "[181] From this it looks as though either we have forgotten the language of the unconscious, or have not yet learned it. Cicero's words are rather fitting here: *etenim qui secum loqui poterit sermones alterius non requiret* (And anyone able to talk with himself does not need to talk with others. Tusc. V 10,117.) In another experience, one of my patients lapsed one day into what can only be described as a state of emergency.[182] It was what is known in French psychiatry as *automatisme ambulatoire*. For about thirty hours she underwent very profound inner experiences which were so powerful that they threatened to tear her apart. Finally she found protection on a manhole cover (mandala form ◎) and was able to find her way back to me. From this moment on she was able to understand her own dreams directly, and she retained this ability; this side effect still does not help us answer the question of whether it was a progressive learning effect or a regressive returning to primary knowledge. The Jungian concept of amplification seems to speak in favor of the second alternative, in that when it comes to the clarification of a dream motif, it falls back on ancient mythological images, in other words it uses a regressive technique.

True, these experiences are rather rare, but even so, the most neutral conclusion cannot be brushed aside, nor is there any mistaking its main meaning, namely that they are a definite indication of the fact that dreams really *do* have a *meaning*. If we have to work out this meaning, then it should help us to think about what possible techniques are at our disposal.

As we are following C. G. Jung as our *homo idoneus*, we shall now describe the conditions which he regards as indispensable in his seminars for a proper treatment of a dream text.

1. *The dreamer's conscious situation should be described.* This means not only the inner situation, insofar as the dreamer is aware of it, but also the external situation.

2. *The dreamer's experiences preceding the dream must be described.* This is an extension of (1) with special emphasis on the events important to the dreamer. It is clear that the indications

gained thereby are of importance for recognizing "remnants of the day" as well as for embedding certain dream elements in the context of the conscious.

3. *The subjective context to the elements of the dream must be established*. *Contextus* (lat.) is the connecting in the active, and the connection in the passive. The context of a passage of writing is established to make it clear where it lies in the train of thought. The dreamer thus supplies the context by informing us what connection a certain dream element has to the contents of his consciousness that he was already aware of. The necessity of this procedure is established by the characteristics of the dream expression as described above (in Chapter IV).

4. *When archaic motifs appear, they call for mythological parallels*. We are now in the field of amplification in the narrowest sense of the term. Of course, there is no point in bringing in *ad libitum* material which may fit in the formal sense. True, it may happen that a dreamer has to be presented with a large selection of such parallels. The decisive factor will always be whether *one* specific mythological parallel makes sense to him, and whether the dream motif makes *him* suddenly see the light of day. As we have already stated, this is an exclusively subjective criterion. We can safely say that whatever is found will come from the cultural background of the dreamer in the broadest sense of the term.

5. *Should they be dreams that occur during analysis, it may be that the analyst's own psychic contents must be brought in*. The theoretical basis for this lies in the observations based on experience that the psyche of the analyst is not irrelevant for what is constellated in the analysand's unconscious. Some extreme examples of this sort of thing have been described in modern times by E. Servadio[183] and by Ian Ehrenwald.[184] Both writers are of the opinion, and with good reasons, that these are cases of parapsychological phenomena, insofar as no known channel can be found on which the information transferred could have got from the analyst to the analysand. This would mean it was telepathy.

The next analogy is, of course, hypnosis, where such things are nothing new. But in contrast to the conscious, active intention of the hypnotizer, the activity of the "sender" in our cases is completely unconscious, which is why we have preferred the model of the interaction of the two unconscious systems. By the way, examples of this can often be observed in everyday life where there are intensive intellectual relationships or discussions—which does not make the matter any less puzzling.

Given these manifestations, it seems to me that the parapsychological hypothesis is the most neutral one, although it provides no explanation. In analytical practice these manifestations are called the special phenomena of "transference and countertransference," a very complicated matter, but this is not the place to discuss it.[185] Sometimes in such situations we get the simultaneous appearance in the environment of physical phenomena (cf. C. G. Jung, *Memories, Dreams, Reflections*[186]), with the result that there has been speculation as to whether paranormal healings, which are common occurrences in special places of pilgrimage or with people with charismatic gifts, do not have some connection with these interactions. Jung would have spoken of synchronistic effects here. (The reader is reminded of the fish symbolism in "Synchronicity as a Principle of Acausal Relations."[187]) Looking at our model, the similarity of the contents of the two unconscious systems would be a case of "arrangement" or coincidence, on the occasion of which the archetype that has been roused would have parapsychological effects, and in these cases even paraphysical ones.[188] But how often it will be possible to prove this coincidence when such things happen, i.e., to be aware of it on both sides, is another *question*; in fact, the question arises of whether the parapsychological effect would not be blocked or cancelled if the whole thing were made conscious, which would thus make the paradoxical situation absolute. Yet the point made in (5) should be heeded, if only on the grounds of scientific honesty. One has often heard that the dreams published by Jungians only occur with Jungians, and Jungians sometimes have the feeling that only Freudians have Freudian dreams. Ian Ehrenwald[189] has actually coined his own term for this phenomenon, and talks of "doctrinal compliance." But I do not believe that this allegedly observational fact can be explained so easily, for my experience has been the exact opposite on too many occasions. In particular, I have seen "Jungian" dreams with people who were never in analysis and had never heard of Jung. And this is particularly true with totally uneducated or deformed people to whom the unconscious apparently speaks loud and clear, i.e., can bring into play an unimpaired battery of archetypal images.

6. *As a final stipulation, Jung emphasizes the drawing up of an objective anamnesis.* This bringing in of objective information from a third party is always necessary when the situation is complicated or unclear, or when the analyst has the strong suspicion that there is something the dreamer is withholding, sees wrongly or cannot know.

Examples from a Dream Series

Considering these various points, it is clear that a dream must be noted down in such a way that the origins of all the material are evident at all times. For this reason we suggest the following schema for a careful processing of dreams:

I	II	III	IV	V	VI	VII
Dream text, if possible already divided up into the dramatic schema	Related conscious experiences	Associations, subjective context	Possible mythological parallels	Possible associations of the analyst	Possible information from third parties and objective information	Resulting explanation of the meaning of the dream

It is not difficult to see that columns II to VI also serve as precautions against too much arbitrariness in the explanation. The basic assumptions behind them have been discussed above and we do not see the need for any further theoretical observation. Instead, we shall give some *examples*, still remaining with our patient from Chap. II/2, p. 8. There are certain advantages in sticking with this case:

1. It is closed, so we know how things went.

2. It consists of a complete series of dreams which runs parallel to the recovery process. This is particularly valuable because unfortunately, whatever precautions are taken, there are inevitably too many uncertainties involved in the interpretation of any one single dream. So it does create much more confidence when several dreams by the same dreamer during one specific period of time are available for discussion. Because dreams usually revolve round one common focal point of meaning, there is a reasonably objective possibility of keeping a check on things in that the interpretation of one dream can be compared with that of the preceding, or following dream. Should this comparison reveal similarities or actual identicality, then one can feel that one's interpretation has been confirmed. This leads to a similar schema to the one proposed above

(p. 14) for the amplification method. One is tempted to say that the dreams in a series "amplify" themselves, that they rotate and orbit round the focal point of meaning and that a correct interpretation of the dream would mean a coinciding with his focal point of meaning. Then the series is completed—frequently one learns this from the fact that from then on people cannot remember their dreams for a long time—or else a whole new morphology occurs, with a new focal point of meaning coming to the fore. If one has the opportunity to observe a very long dream series (i.e., over a period of decades), one can see that as these focal points of meaning (i.e., archetypal motifs) progressively replace each other, they do so with a certain regular succession. This is the empirical basis for what Jung calls the individuation process, which is the result of sufficiently extensively pursued consideration of the unconscious processes on the part of the conscious.

3. One apparent disadvantage of our dream series is that the dreamer was so mentally paralyzed that he was in no position to comment on his dreams. At my request he managed to raise the energy to dictate them to his wife. Thus Columns II and III of our formula do not apply to him. In this case we are thus dealing with perfectly autonomous statements from the unconscious, which in turn justifies our making up for the gaps in Columns II and III by bringing in objective material ourselves, i.e., trying to supplement the lack of subjective information by objective amplification on the lines of Columns IV and V.

4. Moreover, it is advantageous didactically if we do not need to produce for each dream what can often be an endless supply of material from Columns II and III. Material in those columns actually corresponds to the domain of Freudian interpretation, which remains valid in its own right, and knowledge of which is taken for granted. Here, however, we are dealing exclusively with Jungian contributions to the dream. The way the patient lived was incredibly monotonous anyway, as befitted his condition. And therapeutic measures were practically impossible as in those days there were still no pharmacological drugs. Whatever happened, and apparently a lot happened, could only be deduced autonomously and exclusively from the dreams, the patient's only spontaneous activity.

Dream 1

Bearing these remarks in mind, we feel justified in working on the dream in the following way. So let us repeat *Dream 1* and divide it up into the dramatic schema:

(a) *Place, time, dramatis personae*:
"I was fishing for trout, not in a river or lake but in a reservoir that was divided into compartments."

Reservoir divided into compartments.
Present.
Dreamer, finding trident and fish.

(b) *Desis (exposition, "tying the knot")*:
"With ordinary tackle, flies, etc. I had no luck."

No success fishing in the traditional way.

(c) *Krisis (peripetia, change)*:
"I got exasperated and picked up a trident that was lying there."

Emotionalism (exasperation) makes him see more primitive equipment, a trident (*deus ex machina*).

(d) *Lysis (solution)*:
"and immediately succeeded in spearing a splendid fish."

He thus gets a fine catch.

Commentary on Dream 1

With unsurpassable brevity and clarity (a) describes the real-life situation of the deeply melancholy patient: total stagnation, lack of communication (separate compartments, the term for this being "compartment psychology"), nothing is "going on" (flowing). Accordingly his efforts in (b) to catch something in these unfortunately all too "still waters" (of the unconscious) (i.e., to raise their contents (fish) to consciousness), are unsuccessful.

A new element crops up in (c) in the form of exasperation. He feels emotion, which in his state of total apathy must be regarded as beneficial. This change leads to the trident coming into his field of vision, and he picks it up (i.e., becomes active), and uses it as a spear for fishing. This is a regressive use of means, all the more so as the patient was in reality a passionate fisherman and owned a lot of sophisticated equipment. (d) With this primitive equipment he is at once successful and he manages to bring up a respectable amount (fish) from the unconscious (water) to the conscious level, where it can be made assimilable (edible) and which must undoubtedly have given him satisfaction.

If we choose to understand the dream prognostically, which is often possible with initial dreams, it would herald the patient's transformation from a long-lasting vacuum and stagnation into a successful normal state, which was later clinically confirmed. One could declare it a healing dream and here the trident seems to appear spontaneously from the unconscious (dream) as a *deus ex machina* and means of healing. One could leave it with these few relatively harmless expressions and regard the extensive comments on the Poseidon mythology given earlier on as an idle pastime. But the patient reader will have been struck by the fact that almost every detail in the list of mythological features fits the case perfectly in its way, which, given its complexity, can hardly be dismissed as sheer coincidence. At any rate, we are convinced that this amplification went a long way in helping us to understand this case. So if we had not trodden this lengthy path, it would have been to our detriment. What is more, the healing process was so dramatic that to have evaded its numinous aspect would have been harmful both to oneself and to the patient.

The worst thing that can happen to the psychiatrist in such cases is when he feels as though he himself is a healing god, consciously or unconsciously, which is what Jung calls "inflation." In the case of psychiatric healing it is always advisable, given their complexity and their almost miraculous nature, to adopt as many approaches as possible. Mythological and religious models have always had and still have a prominent place here and have still not been replaced by anything "better." Healing is undoubtedly an archetypal event, a *restitutio ad integrum*, a making whole, as can be seen from its etymology (heal = whole), which is why this dream can be described as a formally archetypal one. As regards the contents, the archetypal image of the trident is best understood as *pars pro toto* of Poseidon. To speculate on the triaina as a symbol of the Trinity (e.g., harmony of body, mind and soul) is, like many other things, a matter of taste. Amplifications are only meaningful as part of the whole clinical picture.

Dream 2

1. Text (the division into paragraphs is given in accordance with the division into the phases of the dramatic schema):

(*b*) "The dream began as I dropped my glasses and they broke."

(*c*) "I immediately got into a Ford car that was standing there, and drove to the optician's (I never drive in real life). On the way there I saw an old man, a valued friend and advisor of mine. I asked him to come with me, which he did."

(*d*) "On the way to the optician's I told the old man about my worries and difficulties and got a lot of good advice from him."

And now the application of the dramatic schema to this example:

(*a*) Place: street; time: the present; dramatis personae: dreamer, old man.

	II	III	IV
(*a*) Street, the present, dreamer, old man.	Feels a little better since Dream 1	The brackets in part (*c*)	See Koran passage below
(*b*) Mishap with glasses.			
(*c*) Drives car himself! Sees friend and takes him along.			
(*d*) Confession and good advice from the old man.			

Koran 18 Suras 59–81:

59. Remember when Moses said to his servant, "I will not stop till I reach the confluence of the two seas, or for years will I journey on." 60. But when they reached their confluence, they forgot their fish, and it took its way in the sea at will. 61. And when they had passed on, said Moses to his servant, "Bring us our morning meal; for now have we incurred weariness from this journey." 62. He said, "What thinkest thou? When we repaired to the rock for rest I forgot the fish; and none but Satan made me forget it, so as not to mention it; and it hath taken its way in the sea in a wondrous sort." 63. He said, "It is this we were in quest of." And they both went back retracing their footsteps. 64. Then found they one of our servants to whom we had vouchsafed our mercy, and whom we had instructed with our knowledge. 65. And Moses said to him, "Shall I follow thee that thou teach me, for guidance, of that which thou too hast been taught?" 66. He said, "Verily, thou canst not have patience with me; 67. How canst thou be patient in matters whose meaning thou comprehendest not?" 68. He said, "Thou shalt find me patient if God please, nor will I disobey thy bidding." 69. He said, "Then, if thou follow me, ask me not of aught until I have given thee an account thereof." 70. So they both went on, till they embarked in a ship, and he—*the unknown*—staved it in. "What!" said Moses, "hast thou staved it in that thou mayest drown its crew? a strange thing now hast thou done!" 71. He said, "Did I not tell thee that thou couldst not have patience with me?" 72. He said, "Chide me not that I forgat, nor lay on me a hard command." 73. Then went they on till they met a youth, and he slew him. Said Moses, "Hast thou slain him who is free from guilt of blood? Now hast thou wrought a grievous thing!" 74. He said, "Did I not tell

thee that thou couldst not have patience with me?" 75. Moses said, "If after this I ask thee aught, then let me be thy comrade no longer; but now hast thou my excuse." 76. They went on till they came to the people of a city. Of this people they asked food, but they refused them for guests. And they found in it a wall that was about to fall, and he set it upright. Said Moses, "If thou hadst wished, for this thou mightest have obtained pay." 77. He said, "This is the parting point between me and thee. But I will first tell thee the meaning of that which thou couldst not await with patience. 78. As to the vessel, it belonged to poor men who toiled upon the sea, and I was minded to damage it, for in their rear was a king who seized every ship by force. 79. As to the youth his parents were believers, and we feared lest he should trouble them by error and infidelity. 80. And we desired that their Lord might give them in his place a child, better than he in virtue, and nearer to filial piety. 81. And as to the wall, it belonged to two orphan youths in the city, and beneath it was their treasure: and their father was a righteous man: and thy Lord desired that they should reach the age of strength, and take forth their treasure through the mercy of thy Lord. And not of mine own will I have done this. This is the interpretation of that which thou couldst not bear with patience."

Commentary on Dream 2

It took place in the night after Dream 1. Given the clinical condition of the dreamer, there were no associations or information forthcoming about the dream. In this respect the brackets in part (c) are a step forward. The glasses represent his way "of seeing things," which for years has been dark and bleak. He no longer identifies with them quite so much but has become careless and drops them so that they break. The glasses probably correspond to the conventional fishing tackle in Dream 1, i.e., his depressive outlook on life, which he throws away in the first dream and drops in the second. In other words, he needs "new glasses." To this end he visits the optician, the expert on sight. As it is urgent he decided to go there by car, driving himself, thus becoming active in a hitherto despised function, for in reality he was always driven by his chauffeur. Once again we have here a regressive development, as in Dream 1, and the fact that the vulgar Ford (also regressive) is just standing there corresponds to the lapidary appearance or simple presence of the primitive trident in Dream 1. The Ford model T, which is what it was as we later found out, is the very prototype of the American car, a sort of archetypal car. It thus reminds us of Neptune's chariot and the horses created by Poseidon, as it is measured in terms of hp (horsepower). The fact that the patient takes the wheel himself speaks for itself and represents a remarkable activation, which presupposes that he has already dropped certain outdated prejudices (glasses). The optician, who does not actually appear but is there *in potentia*, probably stands for the analyst.

As can be seen, this manner of observation is a *comparison of motifs* and reveals certain similarities in the way the two dreams go and the elements they contain: failure (fishing), mishap (glasses), helpful elements appearing (trident, fish, Ford, friend). He acquires (catches) the last-mentioned or they come (back) to him spontaneously, and they seem to represent parts of the soul with which contact had been lost. We also carry out this same comparison of motifs with our mythological amplifications from the Koran. However, in the search for a parallel for the "good friend," "old man" and "advisor," our association first went to the fish, for, as will be seen, there are many secrets lurking behind this symbol, and the fish motif recurred much more frequently in the patient's dreams than one would expect even in the most enthusiastic fisherman (*piscator pisces somniat*). But the fact that the fish, and the helpful friend met on the street are connected with each other is no coincidence, as can be seen from the 18th Sura, where both elements are closely connected.

"One of our servants" appears in the place of the revived and lost fish, and as can be seen from literature, this servant *is* the same fish. He is Khidr, the teacher of wisdom ("a lot of good advice") in Sufism, the Islam mysticism. It is said of him that he is the advisor and helper that one meets on the street. The Koran legend is a highly syncretistic text, which is even more unadulterated in the Alexander novel. There the hero, the cook of Alexander the Great, is washing a salted fish in a stream. The fish comes alive and swims away. The cook realizes from this that the stream is the much sought-after stream of life that he has discovered and he drinks of it. Afterwards he and Alexander cannot find the stream again, which is why the "Dhulqarnein" throws him into the sea with a millstone round his neck. Since then, as he is immortal, he has been a sea demon, but also the "guardian of the sea" and Khawwad albuhur, who crosses the sea. So there is quite a lot of similarity with Poseidon. The next parallel is in Jewish mysticism (Kabbalah)— Elias. At any rate he is a being who is very familiar with the sea, the unconscious. It must be regarded as progressive that he changed from the theriomorphous (fish) to the anthropomorphous form.

The mystic doctrine of wisdom taught by Khidr in the Koran legend fits very well with the wise advisor in the dream.

So the Koran legend helps us to see connections which might escape someone not familiar with the phenomenology of the unconscious. One could, of course, adopt a purely energetic point of view for such conjectures and say that these are contents of the unconscious which have a potential in the direction of the conscious. The patient's depression would then correspond to a loss of libido which is now about to be compensated for (progression) by the appearance of equivalent contents from the unconscious. It should be clear that this may be just *one* of the many aspects of the matter. But there is no reason why the formal aspect should be neglected.

Dream 3

1. Text:

(*b*) "In this dream I went to the railway station, apparently the main station in Zurich, to collect a large sum of money which I had to take from the station to one of the banks. I had to go to and fro several times, but had arranged for a guard to follow me, keeping at some distance."

(*c*) "After one or two trips I looked round but could not see the guard, so I quickly turned round and went back to the station, where I found the guard sitting on a comfortable bench in a small park. I accused him of neglecting his duty of keeping watch. My language was pretty strong."

(*d*) "His only reply was to say that the arrangement was a stupid one anyway, since there was no risk of being attacked in Zurich."

(*a*) Place: would consist of station (Zurich), street and bank; time: present, dramatis personae: dreamer and guard.

Commentary on Dream 3

The dream took place on the third night in Zurich. One can say that the patient is now "here" in that he identifies the Zurich main station. From an indefinite distance (the unconscious) large sums of money come to him, available psychic energy (libido). He has to take it to the right place (bank) but is suspicious of his surroundings, a suspicion which corresponds to the still present typical insecurity of the depressive, for he is afraid that he might lose his newly gained energy. But the precautions he feels he has to take do not work, which annoys him. It is possible that the analyst might be hiding behind the bodyguard, in other words that the patient might feel insufficiently protected by him. Faced with such a feeling, the dreamer would have to see from the lysis that this shortcoming is positive in the sense that there is actually a sense of confidence in the situation in Zurich. In this sense the lysis is a comforting one: the suspicion is totally unnecessary, for there are no gangsters in Zurich (that was 1937!). So the bodyguard knows better than the still weak consciousness.

So night after night there came to the patient valuable contents from the unconscious, in three variations: fish, car, advisor and now money. I now ventured to pronounce the favorable prognosis, which was received with the suspicion described above but was not forgotten. The dream situation is now in the almost normal—one could say bourgeois—sphere so that there are no further grounds for mythological amplification. This does not mean that "bourgeois situations" are never archetypal or even mythological. On the contrary, such situations can only be understood properly once those involved can recognize the general human background.

Dream 4

1. Text:

(b) "I was standing on Fifth Avenue in New York, watching the return of the Rainbow Division from the Great War. I saw a lot of old friends among the troops marching past."

(c) "Once the parade was over, some of us met for dinner. In the company was a very humorous officer who was making prophecies about our future. Some of his remarks were very funny."

(d) "He did not get as far as me with his prophecies because the dream ended before."

(a) Place: New York, Fifth Avenue and restaurant; time: 19 years earlier (end of World War I); dramatis personae: dreamer, Rainbow Division, friends, officer.

Commentary on Dream 4

The dreamer is once again on his home territory. The period after World War I had been a high point in his life. He was a member of an international commission and received several decorations. The Rainbow Division had also distinguished itself in the war. (These are all facts that would appear in Columns II and III in more normal conditions; in our case it is thanks to the patient's wife that we have them, so we have to put them in Column VI.) Approximately 10,000 soldiers (instead of the money in Dream 3), who have been engaged in bitter warfare for years, return home and find peace. This means that the nerve-wracking inner struggles of melancholy that have been going on for years and that have held in so much energy (libido) are coming to an end. The microcosmic triumph parade must now be joined more strongly to the ego, which is reinforced by the shared meal (communio). The culmination or peripeteia brings the prophecies of one who "was there," has experience that will lead to the future development. The lysis is once again a disappointment (as in Dream 3) because the waking up prevents it happening. The patient is still ill and one can understand his need for a prognosis, so one wonders why it is not given. Had I promised him too much? Was some bitter blow of fate in store for him that he would not be able to cope with knowing about in his condition? Both questions are refuted by the catamnesis. In my opinion the missing lysis is imperiously directing him to the here and now. He should fully enjoy the return of his strength and accept it as a present from God, the only relevant prophecy.

Dream 5

1. Text:

(b) "I was talking with a lady that I had met here in the hotel (where he was living with his wife). We were at a ball somewhere in Zurich."

(c) "Between dances I asked her to tell me about certain historical events in Switzerland. I was particularly interested in the Habsburg castle. She told me about it in great detail."

(d) "We had just arranged to take a trip there together when the dream ended."

(a) Place: somewhere in Zurich; time: the present; dramatis personae: dreamer, lady.

Commentary on Dream 5

Back in Zurich a lady appears for the first time and he moves with her harmoniously and rhythmically (dancing). This is the first appearance of an anima figure[190] in this series and gives the opportunity to restore living contact with the inner world. This succeeds because of the shared interest in history (the anima often has connections with history and the patient had been very interested in history before, an interest which came back very strongly after his recovery). The Habsburg as "mighty stronghold" is a classical place of refuge. Habsburg = *Habichts* = (hawks), burg (*pyrgos*) = berg = bergen (shelter). Like all typical medieval fortresses it consists of a "Bergfrid" (tower or keep), from "berg" and "frid" = "shelter," and the "pallas." Of course, the "Bergfrid" is also a watchtower. The dreamer's personality certainly has need of such protection. The plan to inspect it provides the lysis, once the contact with the anima has been established by means of the shared interests.

Dream 6

1. Text:

(*b*) "This dream took place in Scotland. A man had been unjustly accused of a crime. He asked me to be his lawyer and to defend him in court."

(*c*) "I did this and the whole court proceedings took place in the dream."

(*d*) "The man was finally acquitted. I was very pleased about this verdict."

(*a*) Place: Scotland; time: the present; dramatis personae: dreamer, accused and judge (scales).

Commentary on Dream 6

The dreamer has a fair amount of Scottish blood. Given this localization one tends to assume that we are dealing here with something hereditary, which reminds one of manic-depressive illnesses. But the man has been *unjustly* accused, so the suspicion must be removed. It is up to the dreamer to do this, and after all he is a lawyer. After putting all his conscious energy into justice (= correct verdict), he wins an acquittal for his alter ego which had been persecuted in its innocence. Part of the lysis is also his satisfaction at what he had achieved; therapeutically it is of no little importance because it shows that he really is affected by inner tendencies toward liberation, as in Dreams 4 and 5 (except that here it is much more spontaneous and more a reaction to his own activity).

Dream 7

1. Text:

"In this dream I experienced the whole dungeon scene from *Fidelio*. I had been to the Opera a couple of evenings earlier and the dream was simply a repetition of what had happened at the Opera House."

(*a*) Place: Zurich, Opera House, dungeon; time: present; dramatis personae: dreamer and figures on the stage.

Commentary on Dream 7

At first glance this dream does not seem to fit into our dramatic schema. Such dreams are fairly common, of course, and one should not interpret anything into them. But it should also be borne in mind that the laconically (depressively) described dungeon scene in *Fidelio* is a highly dramatic one and that to a certain extent the dream text is an ellipsis of this. The dream is also unusual in one other respect: apparently it is a repetition of a real-life experience (visit to the Opera) and nothing else. This contradicts the Jungian rule (see above) according to which dreams are always *variations* of real-life experiences. Now there is a very clear link with the motif in Dream 6, for Florestan is also a wrongly accused prisoner, but this time on the stage. In the section on Aristotle above we discussed the question of how the "drame intérieur" of the dream manages to affect the dreamer and how the cathartic effect works in this respect. In reality the dreamer was almost physically dragged to the Opera by his wife. It could be assumed that in his total apathy he would not be in a position to follow the plot. This seems to be confirmed by the occurrence of the dream if one goes by the theory that the tragedy would have had to have made an impact on him within in order to get to him, to tell him: *Tua res agitur*. In the words of Jeremias Gotthelf:

> While we sleep, the hours go by uncounted, the sleeper is carried away into another country, is raised above the barriers of time and place, walks along special paths on which God himself teaches him with images which come from his fatherly hand, makes him familiar with his weaknesses, makes the happy man taste the cup of unhappiness and comforts the unhappy man with happy dreams; the man who is discontented is conducted to situations that make him contented when he wakes up and ready to take up his old burden once again and bear it with patience. In dreams there is a treasure trove of godly love and wisdom, but few and far between are the souls who are able to take it.[191]

There are striking parallels between the scene from the opera and the patient's depressive state so that actually they should have a shock effect on him. But what was not possible in the theatre was achieved by the dream. As we said earlier, shell-shock dreams are reproductions of the traumatic experience *tale quale*. We said then that there seem to be situations that are not "psychifiable." But perhaps the patient could deal with his situation psychically and hence overcome it if he could see it *sub specie aeternatis*, i.e., as only understandable on the higher level of theatre in the classical sense, where the events acquire an archetypal meaning and are no longer just the troubles of the little man. This function of Dream 7 should be even clearer if one sees the transposition from the Zurich Opera House to the inner stage of the dreamer as a necessary change, brought about by a resolute healing ethos of the unconscious. And even without the catamnesis it should have become clear that this collaboration came from the side of the unconscious here.

To enable the reader to follow these remarks more easily, we now give a brief summary of the dungeon scene in *Fidelio* (1895). This is the whole of the second act, apart from the finale (after the transformation) and is thus the dramatic and musical climax (*Krisis*) and lysis of the actual Bouilly drama:

Act II. In Florestan's dungeon. Florestan alone. In the aria: "In des Lebens Frühlingstagen" ("In Life's Spring Days") he gives moving expression to his love for and trust in Leonore. Overcome by weakness, he sinks back unconscious. Rocco and Leonore enter and start to dig the grave for Florestan (then comes the duet "Nur hurtig fort, nur frisch gegraben" ("Oh hasten now to dig the grave"). Meanwhile Leonore tries to distinguish the features of the prisoner in the half-light. When Florestan wakes up, Rocco gives him a drink of cold water to refresh him. Leonore recognizes her husband's voice as he thanks Rocco. By flattering Rocco, she persuades him to allow her to give Florestan a piece of bread. Pizarro now enters and reveals his identity to Florestan but just as he raises his dagger to strike, Leonore throws herself between them. As Pizarro tries to tear her away, she protects Florestan and, threatening Pizarro with a pistol, she cries out "Töt' erst sein Weib." ("First kill his wife.") The enraged Pizarro has no qualms about committing two murders. Just as one thinks the lives of the two are lost, footsteps are heard. Jaquino enters and announces the arrival of the Minister. Florestan and his wife are saved. In an exultant duet: "O, namenlose Freude" ("O joy beyond all telling") they express their blissful happiness.

We feel that this dream, in its brevity or because of its conciseness, is impressive and understandable enough without analytic processing in the strictest sense of the term, and we also feel that no more examples are needed from the remission phase of this melancholy. But in conclusion we should like to add just one more dream which followed directly on from the complete cure.

Dream 8

"I went to the home of the large male eels in the South Atlantic. I watched billions of eels setting off home and could see them in the water as far as the horizon."

Commentary on Dream 8

To understand this dream properly a number of facts of an objective nature are needed, all of which would belong in Column VI. Although the biology of the eel has been well-known since Johannes Schmidt from the Carlsberg Institute, Copenhagen, did his work, these curious fish have lost none of the enigmatic character that has been theirs since ancient times. Their incredible navigational achievements are still a mystery. Their cycle is briefly as follows[192]: they live in freshwater streams. In autumn some of them stop taking in food and turn into silver eels. They then leave the fresh water, swim into salt water and cross the Atlantic Ocean till they come to the Sargasso Sea southeast of the Bermudas. There they spawn and die. The larva (leptocephali) are transparent and they travel in millions, partly with the help of the Gulf stream, so that after 2 1/2 years they end up back in Europe where they populate the old streams again.

So the biological data in the dream are inaccurate, which is food for thought given the fact that the dreamer was an enthusiastic fisherman. With him the spawning fish have turned into large male eels, whereas in actual fact the male eels are small. Otherwise the overall picture is accurate, if one takes it that the eels swimming back home are glass eels (larva).

The question remains of why the dream makes the males so inaccurately big, when there is a 50 percent chance of getting it right. The unconscious seems to have been out to represent an abundance of the masculine, and one that is so specifically phallic, as a familiar but nonetheless ancient and mysterious process of Nature. Of course the sexual libido was revived with the remission, but it remained perfectly within the norm. Even when this makes us think of Silberer's "spermatazoon dreams,"[193] the meaning of this motif does not ultimately change. When these male, life-renewing forces "find their way home" then the continuation of life is assured. Actually few of these millions reach their destination, but that is enough to meet Nature's needs. I should like to leave it open as to whether or not we have understood this dream. What is important is the image itself, which represents a cyclical process of Nature in its overwhelming greatness and imbues it with the aspect of a natural wonder.

EPILOGUE

Thou hast proved mine heart.
Thou hast visited me in the night.
—Psalm 17,3

The psalmist gives us another concept of the dream, and that is that God examines us while we are asleep. This divine investigation can only be directed at our true being. But it cannot happen without self-awareness and we are not told directly how this is to be gained, for dreams speak in foreign tongues. Can it be that this is actually their way of prompting us to examine ourselves? This would be an obvious conclusion when one fully realizes that there has hardly ever been an age or a people, either primitive or highly cultured, that has not used whatever resources it had to deal with the religious aspect of the numinous dream. When the gods were stripped of their divine nature, dreams started to lose their mystery. The "Acheronta" were stirred up and the whole tremendously complicated phenomenon was reduced to a hypothetical drive with its own destiny. The dream thus became the victim of the so-called scientific world, became its playground in fact.

In Jung's conception of life, however, the dream has the same ranking as it does with the psalmist. Small wonder that we do not understand the dream when we do not understand ourselves. Or: those who do not take their dreams seriously do not take themselves seriously. This conclusion calls for some sort of commentary: too many people take themselves too seriously. All this means is that they take their conscious intentions at their face value and thus overestimate themselves. In business life there is no doubt that this is the right and proper attitude, and there is no room for uncertainty

136

here. But where is the individual who can indulge in the luxury of doubting the businessman within him? And if he does manage to do this, who is the good friend and advisor who fills his mind with these doubts?

In psychological terms we would join Jung in speaking here of the "self." The phrase "Dreams come from the self" would be very consistent with Jung's ideas. But we have not brought it in yet because that would trigger off a fundamental discussion on what the term "self" means, and that does not fall within the scope of this volume. Let the following remarks suffice here: the self is an archetype; it arranges the images and the objects, sometimes *extra corpus*; it is autonomous with regard to consciousness and transcends it; it is the archetype with the greatest numinosity; it plays a central role in religious symbolism (one only has to think of the cross in the West or the mandala in the East, together with its sisters in the West).

In the course of an individuation process, symbols of the self appear more and more frequently in dreams and in a way take over the leadership. So who or what is this so-called self? Or, to phrase it differently: why do theologians complain so much about psychologism when psychological findings are being described? Or have they provided us with the anatomical substrata for the localization of God in man or the psychological foundations for His manifestation in the soul? And on the other hand, scientists dismiss Jung as a mystic and academic circles make the sign of the Cross in front of him because, for example, he approached the phenomenon of the dream very seriously, much more seriously than Freud, who was also "unto the Jews a stumbling-block and unto the Greeks foolishness."[194] For Jung's interpretation of the dream "on the subjective level" means that there is no more evading implacable self-awareness.

So this is where the businessman would have to look for his "friend and advisor," if he did not have enough problems already. And it always needs a "force majeure," of which there are quite a number. Unfortunately it is then somewhat late, for the environment has already had to pay a high price.

And this is where a serious objection arises: who today has the necessary tranquillity and the necessary funds to afford this expenditure? And furthermore: who really knows all the ins and outs of this controversial field, which is so open to arbitrariness and prejudice? And the particularly dangerous attitude: it's OK for those who are crazy, but I'm normal and I don't want to be made crazy! This argument is particularly insidious in that the fundamentals of dream psychology actually do derive from experience with sick people, as we have stressed several times already. But the sick psyche is still a human one and it is just that the illness makes it possible for the psychic principles to be observed under the microscope, as it were. Physiology, too, has been provided with important new ideas from clinical pathology, and the clinic has been able to confirm or correct its extrapolations. At any rate, nobody has been made ill by physiology.

Many more counter-arguments could be brought against the dream hypothesis, but we regard this as futile for we naturally, being what we are, would come up with a final analytical trick of the trade and claim that all these counter-arguments are based on a sort of moral rejection and this also applies to taking responsibility for things which, thank God, were "only a dream," as we so often say with visible satisfaction when we wake up. But self-awareness is the highest demand that can be made on one. Why this is so is clearly not a question to pose to the psychologist. If I do consult him he may at most feel morally obliged to help me in my endeavors. But he can only fulfill this obligation if he himself has "gone through the mill" because—and this is the important thing—it is not enough just to attend to one's dreams; the decisive factor is the conscious deployment of all the forces available to come to terms with the findings that emerge from the raw material so that the consciousness differentials of Leibniz can finally be integrated into a fuller and greater consciousness.

> Gestaltung, Umgestaltung
> des ewgen Sinnes ewge Unterhaltung.
> —Goethe

NOTES

1. Goethe is quoting Purkinje here, cf. note 30.
2. (a) C. G. Jung, "The Psychology of Dreams," Chap. XII of *Collected Papers on Analytical Psychology*, London, 1916, pp. 299–311. This speech has never been published in German. (b) "Allgemeine Gesichtspunkte zur Psychologie des Traumes," in *Ueber die Energetik der Seele* (*Psychol. Abh.* II), Zürich, 1925, and *CW* 8. (c) "Die praktische Verwendbarkeit der Traumanalyse," in *Wirklichkeit der Seele,* Zürich, 1934, and *CW* 16. (d) "Vom Wesen der Träume," *Ciba Z. Nr.* 99, Basel, 1945, pp. 3546–3557, and *CW* 8.
3. Calvin S. Hall and Robert Van der Castle, *The Content Analysis of Dreams*, New York, 1966.
4. S. Freud, *The Interpretation of Dreams*, in Standard Edition, IV and V, London, 1953.
5. Cf. C. A. Meier, "A Jungian View," in *Dream Psychology and the New Biology of Dreaming*, ed. Milton Kramer, Springfield, Ill., 1969.
6. W. v. Siebenthal, *Die Wissenschaft vom Traum*. Berlin, 1953.
7. E. Aserinsky and N. Kleitman, "Regularly Occurring Periods of Eye Motility and Concomittant Phenomena During Sleep," *Science* 118, pp. 273–274, 1953.
8. W. Dement and N. Kleitman, "Cyclic Variations in EEG During Sleep and Their Relation to Eye Movements, Bodily Motility and Dreaming," *Electroenceph. Clin. Neurophysiol.* 9, pp. 673–690, 1957.
9. Niels Bohr, "Licht und Leben," *Die Naturwissenschaften* 21, pp. 245ff., Berlin, 1933.
10. W. Pauli, "Die philosophische Bedeutung der Idee der Komplementarität," in *Experientia* VI/2, Basel, 1950, pp. 72ff.
11. Fr. Wilh. Jos. von Schelling, *Werke I*, 3, Augsburg, 1858, p. 600.
12. E. Kraepelin, *Die Sprachstörungen im Traum*, Leipzig, 1906.
13. K. Leonhard, *Die Gesetze des normalen Träumens*, Leipzig, 1939 and 1952.
14. R. Bossard, *Psychologie des Traumbewusstseins*, Zürich, 1951.
15. C. G. Jung, *Dream Symbols of the Individuation Process*, *CW* 12.
16. C. G. Jung, *Psychology and Alchemy*, *CW* 12.
17. I gave a classical example of amplification in my essay "Ancient Incubation and Modern Psychotherapy," Evanston, 1967.
18. K. Kerényi, *The Gods of the Greeks*, Thames and Hudson, London, 1959.

19. W. H. Roscher, *Ausführliches Lexikon der griechischen und römischen Mythologie*, Leipzig, 1884–93.

20. Cf. my essay referred to in note 17.

21. Our "George." Our Saint George was also called upon by the original Semites of the Near East as Mâr Dschirdschi for the curing of female sterility. Cf. S. J. Curtiss, *Ursemitische Religion im Volksleben des heutigen Orients*, translated into German by W. Graf Baudissin, Leipzig, 1903, p. 123.

22. Heinrich Zimmer, *Abenteuer und Fahrten der Seele*, Zurich, 1961, pp. 249ff.

23. For further details see my previously quoted work (note 17) on Asklepios, the chthonic healing god with whom there are strong resemblances, and whose main attribute, the snake, is just as phallic as Poseidon's trident.

24. For further details see C. G. Jung and Wolfgang Pauli: *The Interpretation of Nature and the Psyche*, Pantheon, New York, 1955, and *CW* 8.

25. Judd Marmor, "Limitations of Free Association," *Arch. Gen. Psychiat.*, 22, pp. 160–65, 1970.

26. Marmor, "Psychoanalytic Therapy as an Educational Process," in ed. J. Masserman, *Science and Psychoanalysis*, Vol. 5, pp. 286ff., New York, 1962.

27. Marmor, "Psychoanalytic Therapy and Theories of Learning," ibid., Vol. 7, pp. 265ff., New York, 1964.

28. S. Freud, Selbstdarstellung. 2. Aufl. p. 54, Wein 1936.

29. Betty Heimann, "Die Tiefschlafspekulation der alten Upanishaden," in *Untersuchungen zur Geschichte des Buddhismus* VII, p. 20, Zs. f. Buddhismus, Munich, 1922.

30. J. E. Purkinje, "Wachen, Schlaf und verwandte Zustände," in *Handwörterbuch der Physiologie mit Rüchsicht auf physiologische Pathologie*, ed. Rudolf Wagner III./2, pp. 412–480, Braunschweig, 1846.
Purkinje is one of the greatest physiologists and pathologists of his day and achieved world-wide renown through his description of
1. The retina blood vessels (Purkinje vein figure)
2. The germ layer in a bird's egg (Purkinje blister)
3. The Purkinje phenomenon, the well-known fact that in the twilight the blue color subjectively grows brighter compared to the others (l'heure bleue)
4. The ganglion cells of the cerebellum (Purkinje cells) and also
5. The axis cylinder of the nerve fibres.
We shall come back to Purkinje later. Purkinje's works on sight opened up new roads and were lavishly praised by Goethe, who examined them thoroughly in 1819.

31. Ian Oswald, *Sleeping and Waking*, Amsterdam/New York, 1962.

32. S. Freud, cf. note 4 above.

33. P. Jessen, *Versuch einer wissenschaftlichen Begründung der Psychologie*, Berlin, 1856.

34. G. F. Meier, *Versuch der Erklärung des Nachtwandelns*, Halle, 1758.

35. A. Maury, *Le sommeil et les rêves*, Paris 1861.

36. S. Freud, cf. note 4 above.

37. A. Maury, ibid., pp. 139ff., 3rd ed., Paris, 1865.

38. Heinrich Spitta, *Die Schlaf- und Traumzustände der menschlichen Seele*, Freiburg i.B., 1892, 2nd ed., p. 283.

39. Cf. Georg Jacob, *Märchen und Traum*, Hannover 1923.

40. John Mourly Vold, *Über den Traum*, 2 vols., ed. O. Klemm, Leipzig, 1910 and 1912.

41. S. Freud, cf. note 4 above.

42. S. Freud, ibid.

43. S. Freud, ibid.

44. Johannes Müller, *Üeber die phantastischen Gesichtserscheinungen*, Coblenz, 1836, republished with a commentary by Ulrich Ebbecke, Hannover, 1951, and as a reprint with Werner Fritsch, Munich, 1967.

45. George Trumbull Ladd, "Contribution to the Psychology of Visual Dreams," *Mind*, April, 1892.

46. Herbert Silberer, "Symbolik des Erwachens und Schwellensymbolik überhaupt," *Jb. psychoanal. psychopathol.* Forschgg. III. pp. 621 ff., Leipzig and Wien, 1912.

47. Ibid. p. 625.

48. Herbert Silberer, *Der Traum*, Stuttgart, 1919, pp. 10ff.

49. Ludwig Strümpell, *Die Natur und Entstehung der Träume*, Leipzig, 1874, p. 107.

50. S. Freud, cf. note 4 above.

51. Karl Schrötter, "Experimentelle Träume," *Zbl. Psychoanal.* II, Wiesbaden, 1912, pp. 638–646.

52. K. Schrötter, l.c., pp. 638 and 641.

53. K. Schrötter, l.c., pp. 644 and 645.

54. K. A. Scherner, *Das Leben des Traumes*, Berlin, 1861.

55. Ibid. p. 242.

56. Ibid. p. 116.

57. Ibid. pp. 118ff.

58. Ibid. p. 120.

59. Ibid. p. 123.

60. Ibid. pp. 121ff.

61. Ibid. p. 207.

62. Ibid. p. 166.

63. J. G. Graber and J. G. Gichtel, *Eine kurtze Eröffnung und Anweisung Der dreyen Principien und Welten Im Menschen*, In unterschiedlichen Figuren vorgestellt, o.O. 1696.

64. Tobia Nerol, *Sepher Haolamoth sive Opus encyklopaedicum tripertitum Hebraice*, Venedig, 1707–08. Nerol was the first Jew to be allowed to attend a German university (Frankfurt, a.O.). He was the first person to describe the "plica polonica."

65. Ottavio Scarlatini, *Dell'huomo figurato e simbolico*, Bologna, 1684. Cf. also Carl Hentze, *Das Haus als Weltort der Seele*, Stuttgart, 1961.

66. C. G. Jung, "Association, Dream and Hysterical Symptom: Diagnostic Association Studies VIII." *Journ. Psychol. Neurol.*, Vol. 8, Leipzig, 1906, pp. 25–60, and *CW* 2.

67. C. A. Meier, *The Unconscious in its Empirical Manifestations*, Boston, 1984, pp. 120–122.

68. H. Silberer, "Lekanomantische Versuche," *Zbl. Psychoanal.* II, pp. 383ff., 438ff., 518ff. and 566ff., Wiesbaden, 1912; "Zur Charakteristik des lekanomantischen Schauens," *Zbl. Psychoanal.* III, pp. 73ff., 129ff., Wiesbaden, 1912.

69. Silberer was also a predecessor of Jung through his studies on "Probleme der Mystik und ihrer Symbolik," Wien and Leipzig, 1914, in which he was the first to deal with alchemical symbolism.

70. H. Silberer, "Zur Charakteristik des lekanomantischen Schauens," *Zbl. Psychoanal.* III, p. 76, Wiesbaden, 1912.

71. H. Silberer, ibid., pp. 97–98.
72. C. A. Meier, H. Rüf, A. Ziegler, and C. S. Hall, "Forgetting of Dreams in the Laboratory," *Perceptual and Motor Skills*, 1968, 26, pp. 551–557.
73. C. S. Hall and R. L. Van de Castle, *The Content Analysis of Dreams*, New York, 1966.
74. Cf. C. A. Meier, note 17 above.
75. C. G. Jung, "Synchronicity: An Acausal Connecting Principle," *CW* 8.
76. Cf. J. T. Shurley, "Profound Experimental Sensory Isolation," *Am. Journ. Psychiat.* 117, 1960, p. 539.
77. There is a compilation that is easily available on the role of the dream in more than 10 different cultures: *The Dream and Human Societies*, ed. G. E. von Grunebaum and Roger Caillois, Berkeley and Los Angeles, 1966.
78. A. Leo Oppenheimer, "The Interpretation of Dreams in the Ancient Near East," *Transact. Amer. Philos. Soc.*, New Series, Vol. 46, Part 3, Philadephia, 1956.
79. E. L. Ehrlich, "Der Traum im Alten Testament," *Beihefte zur Zs. atliche. Wissenschaft*, 73, Berlin, 1953. Cf. also Joshua Trachtenberg, *Jewish Magic and Superstition*, Atheneum Book 15, New York, 1974, esp. his bibliography, p. 309.
80. H. Schär, "Bemerkungen zu Träumen der Bibel," in *Traum und Symbol, neuere Arbeiten zur analytischen Psychologie C. G. Jung*, ed. C. A. Meier, Zürich, 1963, pp. 171ff.
81. Ramanuja, Siddhanta, "Ein Kommentar zu den Brahmasutras, zugänglich durch Rudolf Ottos Übersetzung" in *Religiöse Stimmen der Völker. Die Religion des alten Indien* III/II, Jena 1917.
82. E. Abegg, *Indische Psychologie*, Zürich, 1945.
83. Julius von Negelein, "Der Traumschlüssel des Jagaddeva," *Religions-geschichtliche Versuche und Vorarbeiten*, ed. R. Wünsch and L. Deubner, XI/4, Giessen, 1912.
84. Cf. my representation of the analogous Greek motif in C. A. Meier, note 17.
85. Ibid.
86. Ibid.
87. Mary Hamilton, *Incubation or the Cure of Disease in Pagan Temples and Christian Churches*, London, 1906.
88. C. A. Meier, "Zeitgemässe Probleme der Traumforschung," *Kultur-Staatswiss. Schrr. E.T.H.*, 75, Zürich, 1950, p. 19.
89. F. A. Wolf, *Vermischte Schriften und Aufsätze in lateinischer und deutscher Sprache*, Halle, 1802, p. 385.
90. Cf. Karl Reinhardt, *Platons Mythen*, Bonn, 1927, a highly recommended book in which, among others, there is the following sentence related to our subject (p. 46): "Denn in dem Grade, wie die Seele selbst in die Spekulation über die Seele eindringt—und ganz fehlt dies bei Platon nie—wird die Spekulation über die Seele selbst zum Seelen-Mythos." ("For to the extent that the soul itself permeates the speculation on the soul—and that is never far away with Plato, the speculation on the soul becomes itself the soul myth.")
91. Cicero, *Gedanken über Tod und Unsterblichkeit*, ed. Klaus Reich, Hans Günter Zekl, Klaus Bringmann, Bd. 273, Hamburg, 1969; better in Raffaello del Re, M. T. Ciceronis Somnium Scipionis, in *Nova biblioteca dei Classici Greci e Latini*, ed. G. Ugolini, Firenze, 1962.
92. *Collection des auteurs latins*, ed. M. Nisard, Paris, 1883.
93. Wm. Harris Stahl, *Macrobius, Commentary on the Dream of Scipio*, New York, 1952.

94. Matthaeus Schedler, *Die Philosophie des Macrobius und ihr Einfluss auf die Wissenschaft des christlichen Mittelalters.* Beiträge zur Geschichte der Philosophie des Mittelalters, Texte und Untersuchungen, ed. Clemens Baeumker XIII I, Münster i.W. 1916.

95. Hugo Linke, "Über Macrobius' Kommentar zu Ciceros Somnium Scipionis," in *Philol. Abh.*, Martin Hertz zum 70. Geburtstag von ehemaligen Schülern dargebracht, Berlin, 1888, pp. 240–256. Cf. also Richard Mansfield Haywood, *Studies on Scipio Africanus,* Greenwood Press, London, 1933.

96. Maurice Henry-Couannier, *Saint François de Sales et ses amitiés,* 5me édition, Paris-Bruxelles, 1956, pp. 281ff.

97. My thanks are due to Elisabeth Rüf, Ph.D., for this information.

98. Migne, *Patrol. Graec. Lat. tom.* 66, 1281ff.

99. Richard Volkmann, *Synesius von Kyrene,* Berlin, 1869.

100. Joh. Geffcken, *Der Ausgang des griechisch-römischen Heidentums,* Heidelberg, 1920.

101. W. Lang, *Das Traumbuch des Synesius von Kyrene,* Tübingen, 1926. The best representation today: C. Lacombrade, *Synesios de Cyrène,* Paris, 1951.

102. Cf. in this respect particularly Wollenweide, S. *Neuplaonische und christliche Theologie bei Synesios von Kyrene.* 1985. *Forschungen zur Kirchen- und Dogmengeschichte,* 35.

103. His personality is vividly described by Georg Grützmacher, *Synesios von Kyrene. Ein Charakterbild aus dem Untergang des Hellenentums,* Leipzig, 1913. His sufferings with the problematic of time led Stefan Andres to write a novel: *Die Versuchung des Synesios,* München, 1971, as with Charles Kingsley (1819–1875) in his story "Hypatia" (1853). J. Bregman, *Synesius of Cyrene,* philosopher-bishop, 1982.

104. A. Ludwig, "Die Schrift περὶ ἐνυπνίων des Synesius von Kyrene," in *Psychische Studien* XLIII/2–3, Leipzig, 1916.

105. R. Reitzenstein, *Die hellenistischen Mysterienreligionen,* 3rd ed., Leipzig, 1927.

106. H. Leisegang, *Pneuma hagion; der Ursprung des Geistbegriffs der synopt.* Evangelien aus der griech. Mystik, Leipzig, 1922.

107. Cf. my remarks in: "Psychosomatik in Jungscher Sicht," *Psyche* 10, 1962, p. 633.

108. Tertullian deals with this aspect of dreams in Chap. 46 "de anima," where we also find interesting comments on the "soul body" (vehiculum animae) as a subtle, light-like entity.

109. This demand is found already in Aelius Aristides, hieroi logoi I, 3.

110. This belief has totemistic overtones. Unusual behavior of the totem animal in dreams is always interpreted by the aborigines of N.W. Australia as a bad omen. My thanks are due to Rix Weaver, Applecross, W.A., whose verbal comments on this subject are my source of information.

111. Sir John Woodroffe, *The Garland of Letters,* 3rd ed., Madras, 1955.

112. C. G. Jung, "On the Significance of Number Dreams," *Zbl. Psychoanal.* I. Wiesbaden, 1911, pp. 567–572, and *CW* 4, pp. 48ff.

113. Cf. René Allendy, *Le symbolisme des nombres,* Paris, 1921, and Oskar Fischer, *Orientalische und griechische Zahlensymbolik,* Leipzig, 1918, and also the "Cabala del Lotto" in Italy, which describes "buried cultural riches" which still enjoy great popularity in Latin American countries (cf. the game of "Bicho" in Brazil).

114. Artemidori Daldiani, *Onirocritcon Libri v*, ed. Roger A. Pack, Bibliotheca Teubneriana, Leipzig, 1963.

115. *Artemidoros aus Daldis Symbolik der Träume. Übersetzt und mit Anmerkungen begleitet von Friedrich S. Krauss*, Wien, Budapest, Leipzig, 1881. This translation was adapted and extended by M. Kaiser, Basel/Stuttgart 1965.

116. Cf. Nolan D. C. Lewis and Carney Landis, "Freud's Library," *The Psychoanalytic Review*, Vol. 44, 3, p. 351, USA 1957.

Harry Trosman, M.D., and Roger Dennis Simmons, M.A., *Journal of the Am. Psychoanalytic. Assoc.*, Vol. 21, No. 3, 1973. Book section, International Universities Press Inc., N.Y.

117. C. A. Meier, cf. footnote 17.

118. R. Herzog, *Die Wunderheilungen von Epidauros*, Philologus, Supplementband XXII, Heft III, Leipzig, 1931.

119. A. Schopenhauer, *Versuch über Geistersehen und was damit zusammenhängt* (Parerga und Paralipomena).

120. Darius Del Corno, "Graecorum de re oneirocritica scriptorum reliquiae," *Testi e documenti per lo studio dell'Antichità*, vol. XXVI, Milano, 1969.

121. Cf. Lynn Thorndike, *A History of Magic and Experimental Science*, Vol. II, pp. 161ff., New York, 1929.

122. Girolamo Cardano, Somniorum Synesiorum, omnis generis insomnia explicantes, libri IV, Basel 1562. His most important dreams are more easily accessible in the German translation of the autobiography of Cardano, carried out by Hermann Hefele "Des Girolamo Cardano von Mailand (Bürgers von Bologna) eigene Lebensbeschreibung," Jena, 1914. The original publication has the title "De propria vita liber," Gent, 1654. An Italian translation of this book is Gerolamo Cardano, *Autobiografia*, ed. P. Franchetti, Universale Einaudi Nr. 57, Turin, 1945.

122. I.P.V. Troxler, *Blick in das Wesen des Menschen*, 1812.

123. C. A. Eschenmayer, *Psychologie in drei Theilen*, Stuttgart and Tübingen, 1822, p. 227.

124. J.K.F. Rosenkranz, *Psychologie oder die Wissenschaft vom subjektiven Geist*, 1837, 2nd ed., Königsberg, 1843.

125. J. H. Fichte, *Psychologie*, Leipzig, 1864.

126. C. G. Carus, *Vorlesungen über Psychologie*, ed. Edgar Michaelis, 1st ed. 1831, also published Zürich, 1931.

127. C. G. Carus, ibid., p. 293.

128. S. Freud, l.c.

129. W. von Siebenthal, *Die Wissenschaft vom Traum*, Berlin 1953.

130. F. Splittengerber, *Schlaf und Tod*, Halle, 1865.

131. J. E. Purkinje, l.c., p. 467.

132. Cf. Kock, *Com. Att. Frag. II*, p. 442, *Mnesimachos* No. 11.

133. H. Spitta, *Die Schlaf- und Traumzustände der menschlichen Seele*, Freiburg, i.B., 1877.

134. P. Radestock, *Schlaf und Traum*, Leipzig, 1879.

135. Philipp Lersch, *Der Traum in der deutschen Romantik*, München, 1923.

136. A. Béguin, *L'âme romantique et le rêve*, Paris, 1937; 2nd ed. 1963.

137. J. H. Jackson—famous among other things for the Jackson epilepsy named after him.

138. O. Andersson, *Studies in the Prehistory of Psychoanalysis*, Norstedts, 1962, pp. 106ff.

139. *Selected Writings of J. H. Jackson*, ed. James Taylor, 2 vols., London, 1958.

140. Ibid., Vol. 2, pp. 45ff.

141. Ibid., p. 71.

142. P. Janet, *L'état mental des hystériques*, Paris, 1893/94.

143. P. Janet, "Les oscillations du niveau mental," in *Nouveau traité de psychologie*, Tome IV, F. 3, Paris, 1937.

144. P. Janet, *L'état mental des hystériques*, p. 543.

145. P. Janet, "Les oscillations du niveau mental," p. 404.

146. What Man does not know or consider wanders in the night through the labyrinth of the bosom.

147. M. Prince, *The Dissociation of a Personality*, London, 1905.

148. A. Huxley, *The Devils of Loudun*, London, 1952, p. 344; also p. 345.

149. C. G. Jung, "A Review of the Complex Theory," *Kultur- und staatswissenschaftliche Schriften der E.T.H.* Nr. 12, Zürich, 1934, and *CW* 8.

150. C. G. Jung, "On the Nature of Dreams," *CW* 8.

151. C. G. Jung, "On Psychic Energy" and "On the Nature of Dreams," *CW* 8.

152. F. Nietzsche, *Die Geburt der Tragödie*, 1870/71.

153. F. Nietzsche, Menschliches, Allzumenschliches I.12.

154. Aristotle, *Politeia*. VIII, 1344ff.

155. C. A. Meier, "Zeitgemässe Probleme der Traumforschung," *Kultur- und staatswissenschaftliche Schriften der E.T.H.*, Nr. 75, Zürich.

156. A. Stahr, *Aristoteles und die Wirkung der Tragödie*, Berlin, 1859.

157. A. Silberstein, *Die Katharsis des Aristoteles*, Leipzig, 1867.

158. J. Bernays, *Grundzüge der verlorenen Abhandlung des Aristoteles über Wirkung der Tragödie*, Breslau, 1857; later edition, Georg Olms, Hildesheim, 1970.

159. Ibid. p. 42.

160. Ibid. p. 12.

161. Cf. my treatise on "Ancient Incubation and Modern Psychotherapy," Evanston, 1967.

162. Quoted from Bernays, l.c., p. 60.

163. Ibid., pp. 69–70.

164. Talmud babli (Tr. Berachoth 55a)

165. Friedrich Nietzsche, *Morgenröte*, II, 128.

166. The various roles of the term compensation in the broader sense in Jungian psychology are discussed in detail by David Hart, *Der tiefenpsychologische Begriff der Kompensation*, Zürich, 1956, pp. 86ff. (Zürcher Diss.).

167. C. G. Jung, *Psychologische Typen*, Zürich, 1921, p. 674, and *CW* 6 (p. 473 in the Bollingen translation: *Psychological Types*).

168. Cf. Erwin Rousselle, "Spiritual Guidance in Contemporary Taoism," in *Spiritual Discipline*, Pantheon, New York, 1960, pp. 59ff.

169. C. G. Jung, *Psychology and Religion*, New Haven, 1938, and *CW* 11.

170. L. Frobenius, *Das Zeitalter des Sonnengottes*, Berlin, 1904.

171. Comments on "Grimm's Fairy Tales" edited by Johannes Bolte and Georg Polivka, Berlin, 1915–1937, 5 vols.

172. C. G. Jung, "On the Nature of Dreams," *CW* 8.

173. C. A. Meier, *Ancient Incubation and Modern Psychotherapy*, Evanston, 1967, pp. 67–68.

174. R. Wilhelm and C. G. Jung, *The Secret of the Golden Flower*, London and New York, 1962.

175. MS in my possession.

176. Cf. the very interesting book by Julie Eisenbud, *Psi and Psychoanalysis, Studies in the Psychoanalysis of Psi-conditioned Behavior*, New York and London, 1970.

177. J. W. Dunne, *An Experiment with Time*, London, 1927.

178. Id. *The Serial Universe*, London, 1934.

179. C. G. Jung, "On the Psychology and Pathology of So-called Occult Phenomena," *CW* 1.

180. L. Ginzberg, *The Legends of the Jews*, Vol. II, p. 691, Philadelphia, 1954.

181. I thank Riwkah Kluger-Schärf, Ph.D., for this information.

182. Cf. C. A. Meier, "Spontaneous Manifestations of the Collective Unconscious," November 1985.

183. E. Servadio, "Ein paranormaler Traum in der analytischen Situation," *Zs. Parapsychol. Grenzgeb. Psychol. I*, Bern, 1956/58, pp. 155–165.

184. I. Ehrenwald, *New Dimensions of Deep Analysis*, London, 1954.

185. C. A. Meier, "Psychosomatic Medicine from the Jungian Point of View," *Journ. Anal. Psychol.* 8, London, 1963, pp. 103–121.

186. C. G. Jung, *Memories, Dreams, Reflections*, Pantheon, New York, 1963.

187. C. G. Jung, W. Pauli, cf. note 24.

188. C. A. Meier, l.c.

189. I. Ehrenwald, l.c.

190. See Volume IV of this textbook for more details about this term from Jungian psychology.

191. J. Gotthelf, *Jakobs Wanderungen*, Chap. 16, Lützelflühe, 1842.

192. Cf. Leon Bertin, *Eels, A Biological Study*, London 1956, Eng. translation of *Les Anguilles*, Payot, Paris.

193. Herbert Silberer, "Zur Frage der Spermatozoenträume," *Jb. Psychoanal. psychopathol.* Forschungen, Leipzig/Wien, 1912, IV, pp. 708–740.

194. I Cor. I, 23.

BIBLIOGRAPHY

This bibliography makes no attempt to be complete as regards literature on the dream. Lists of this kind are easily available in the latest editions of Freud's *The Interpretation of Dreams* and Von Siebenthal's works. In this list, however, are a certain number of works, in addition to those quoted and discussed in this book, which are necessary reading for an understanding of the Jungian point of view and which have proved valuable in the preparation of this volume without actually being mentioned in the text.

Abegg, E., *Indische Psychologie*. Zurich, 1945.

Abt, L. E., and Riess, B. F., eds., *Dreams and Dreaming*. New York and London, 1968.

Ahlenstiel, H., and Kaufmann, R., *Vision und Traum*. Stuttgart, 1962.

Ahlfeld, F., *Traum und Traumformen; ein Beitrag zur Frage nach der Entstehung des Traumes und seiner Bilder*. Leipzig, 1916.

Ahmad Ibn Sirin, *Apomasaris Apotelesmata, sive de significatis et eventis insomniorum, ex Indorum, Persarum, Aegyptorumque disciplina; depromptus ex Jo*. Sambuci bibliotheca liber, 10. Leunclaio interprete. Frankfort, 1577.

Akert, K., Bally, C., and Schade, J. P., "Sleep Mechanisms," *Progress in Brain Research*, Vol. 18, Amsterdam, London and New York, 1965.

Allendy, R., *Le symbolisme des nombres*. Paris, 1921.

Ambelain, R., *Les visions et les rêves; leur symbolisme prémonitoire*. Paris, 1953.

Andersson, O., *Studies in the Prehistory of Psychoanalysis*. Norstedts, 1962.

Andres, S., *Die Versuchung des Synesios*. Munich, 1971.

Apomasaris Traumbuch. Wittemberg, 1627.

Aristides, Aelius, *hieroi logoi I*.

Aristotle, *Politics*, VIII.
——— *De insomniis et divinatione per somnum*. Leiden, 1947.
Artemidorus and Achmet, Artemidori & Achmetis Sereimi F. oneirocrit-
   ica; Astrampsychi & Nicephori versus etiam oneirocritici; Nicolai Rigal-
   tii ad Artemidorum notae. Lutetiae, 1603.
——— *Traumbuch*. Leipzig, 1677.
——— *Onirocriticon libri 5*. Lipsiae, 1963.
——— *Symbolik der Träume*. Vienna, 1881. New edition, M. Kaiser,
   Basel and Stuttgart, 1965.
Artemidoro Daldiano, *Dell'interpretazione dei Sogni* nella traduzione di
   Pietro Lauro Modenese. Rome, 1970.
Aserinsky, E., and Kleitman, N., "Regularly Occurring Periods of Eye
   Motility and Concomitant Phenomena During Sleep," *Science*, 118,
   1953.
Die Astronomischen Lehrsätze nach lehrende Chiromantie. Frankfort and
   Leipzig, 1746.
Bachelard, G., *Le droit de rêver*. Paris, 1970.
Baust, W., ed., *Ermüdung, Schlaf und Traum*. Stuttgart, 1970.
Becker, R., *The Understanding of Dreams or the Machinations of the
   Night*. London, 1968.
Beguin, A., *L'âme romantique et le rêve*. Paris, 1937, 2nd ed., 1963.
Behn, S. and Lindworsky, J., *Psychologische Methoden der Traumfor-
   schung*. Berlin and Vienna, 1922.
Berger, H., "Uber das Elektroenkephalogramm des Menschen, *Journal
   für Psychologie Neurologie*, 40, 1930.
Bernays, J., *Grundzüge der verlorenen Abhandlung des Aristoteles über
   Wirkung der Tragödie*. Breslau, 1857. Reprint, Hildesheim, 1970.
Bertin, L., *Eels*. London, 1956.
Binswanger, L., *Wandlungen in der Auffassung und Deutung des Traumes
   von den Griechen bis zur Gegenwart*. Berlin, 1928.
Bjerre, P., *Das Träumen als Heilungsweg der Seele*. Zürich and Leipzig,
   1936.
Bohr, N., "Licht und Leben," *Die Naturwissenschaften*, 21, Berlin, 1933.
Bolte, J. and Polivka, G., Anmerkungen zu den Kinder- und Haus-
   märchen der Brüder Grimm. Berlin, 1915–37, five volumes.
Boss, M., *Der Traum und seine Auslegung*. Bern, 1959.
Bossard, R., *Psychologie des Traumbewusstseins*. Zürich, 1951.
Breger, L., "Function of Dreams," *Journal of Abnormal Psychology and
   Social Psychology*. Monograph 72, 1967.
Das Büchlein vom guten Schlaf. Chemische Werke Albert, ed., Leipzig,
   no date.
Büchsenschütz, B., *Traum und Traumdeutung im Alterthume*. Berlin,
   1868.
Calgari, G., *Il sonno e i sogni*. Bologna, 1928.
Cardanus, H., *Somniorum Synesiorum, omnis generis insomnia ex-
   plicantes*, libri iv. Basel, 1562.

Carus, C. G., *Vorlesungen über Psychologie*, ed. Edgar Michaelis, 1831. New edition, Zürich, 1931.

Cassina, U., *Congetture su i sogni*. Parma, 1783.

Cicero, M. T., *Somnium Scipionis*. Florence, 1962.

—— *Gedanken über Tod und Unsterblichkeit*. Hamburg, 1969.

Clodd, E., *Miti e sogni*. Turin, 1905.

Cohn, T. (Tobia Kohen b. [Jirmijja] Moses Nerol.), *Sepher haolamoth s. Opus Tobiae encyklopaedicum tripertitum Hebraice*. Venice, 1707–08.

del Corno, D., *Graecorum de re oneirocritica scriptorum reliquiae*. Milan, 1969.

Curtiss, S. J., *Ursemitische Religion im Volksleben des heutigen Orients*, German by W. Graf Baudissin. Leipzig, 1903.

Delage, Y., *Le rêve; étude psychologique, philosophique et littéraire*. Paris, 1919.

Delboeuf, J., *Le sommeil et les rêves considérés principalement dans leurs rapports avec les théories de la certitude de la mémoire*. Paris, 1885.

Dement, W., and Kleitman, N., "Cyclic Variations in EEG During Sleep and Their Relation to Eye Movement, Body Motility and Dreaming," *Electorenceph. Clin. Neurophysiol.*, 9, 1957.

Dessoir, M., *Das Ich, der Traum, der Tod*. Stuttgart, 1947.

Diamond, E., *The Science of Dreams*. London, 1962.

Documenta Geigy: *Im schatten der Nacht*, five booklets, Basel, 1958–59.
   Booklet 1: (U. Rahm). Das Nachtleben von Urwaldtieren, 1958.
   Booklet 2: (R. Geigy). Nächtliche Blutsauger, 1959.
   Booklet 3: (E. M. Lang). Nächtliches Leben im Zoo, 1959.
   Booklet 4: (A. Portmann). Tierisches Licht im Dunkeln, 1959.
   Booklet 5: (E. Sutter). Der nächtliche Vogelzug, 1959. *Dreams and Self-Knowledge*. London, 1956.

Drummond, J., *Inheritance of Dreams*. London, 1945.

Dunne, J. W., *An Experiment with Time*. London, 1927.

—— *The Serial Universe*. London, 1934.

Du Prel, K., *Gibt es Warnungsträume?* Leipzig, 1893.

Dyroff, A., *Aus schlichten Traumbeobachtungen*. Leipzig, 1930.

Ehrenwald, I., *New Dimensions of Deep Analysis*. London, 1954.

Ehrlich, E. L., "Der Traum im Alten Testament," *Z.f.atliche*. Wissenschaft, Beihefte 73. Berlin, 1953.

Eisenbud, J., *Psi and Psychoanalysis*. New York and London, 1970.

Elferink, M. A., *La descente de l'âme d'après Macrobe*. Leiden, 1968.

Ellis, H., *Die Welt der Träume*. Würzburg, 1911.

Eschenmayer, C. A., *Psychologie in drei Theilen*. Stuttgart and Tübingen, 1822.

Esser, P. H., *Die Welt der Träume*. Konstanz, 1966.

Ettlinger, E., "Precognitive Dreams in Celtic Legend." *Folk-Lore*, LIX, London, 1948.

Fabius, E., *Specimen psychologico-medicum de somniis, quod, annuente summo numine, ex auctoritate rectoris magnifici J. L. C. Schroeder van*

*der Kolk...pro gradu doctoratus...in Academia Rheno-trajectina...
publico ac solemni examini submittit Everardus Fabius.* Amsterdam,
1836.

Fichte, J. H., *Psychologie.* Leipzig, 1864.

Fischer, O., *Orientalische und griechische Zahlensymbolik.* Leipzig, 1918.

Fischgold, H., ed., *Le sommeil de nuit normal et pathologique.* Paris,
1965.

Foucault, M., *Le rêve; études et observations.* Paris, 1906.

Foulkes, D., *Die Psychologie des Schlafes,* Frankfurt, 1969.

Freud, S., *Selbstdarstellung.* 2nd Ed. Vienna, 1936 (*C W* 14 u. 16).

——— *The Interpretation of Dreams.* Standard edition, IV and V, London, 1960. Original German edition, Leipzig and Vienna, 1900.

——— *On Dreams,* New York, 1963. Original German edition, Wiesbaden, 1911.

Frétigny, R., and Virel, A., *L'Imagerie mentale.* Introduction à l'oniro-
thérapie. Geneva, 1968.

Frobenius, L., *Das Zeitalter des Sonnengottes.* Berlin, 1904.

Geffcken, J., *Der Ausgang des griechisch-römischen Heidentums.* Heidelberg, 1920.

Giessler, K. M., *Beiträge zur Phänomenologie des Traumlebens.* Halle
a.S., 1888.

——— *Aus den Tiefen des Traumlebens.* Halle a.S., 1890.

——— *Die physiologischen Beziehungen der Traumvorgänge.* Halle a.S.,
1896.

Ginzberg, L., *The Legends of the Jews,* Vol. ɪɪ, Philadelphia, 1954. 7
volumes. The Jewish Publication Society of America. Translated from
the German M.S. by Henrietta Szold (10th edition), orig. 1909.

Gonseth, J. P., *Théâtre de veille et théâtre de songe.* Neuchâtel, 1950.

Gotthelf, J., *Jakobs Wanderungen.* Lützelflühe, 1842.

Graber, J. G., and Gichtel, J. G., *Eine kurtze Eröffnung und Anweisung
Der dreyen Principien und Welten im Menschen. In unterschiedlichen
Figuren vorgestellet.* 1696.

Green, C. E., *Lucid Dreams.* London, 1968.

Grinstein, A., *On Sigmund Freud's Dreams.* Detroit, 1968.

von Grunebaum, G. E., and Caillois, R., ed., *The Dream and Human Societies.* Berkeley and Los Angeles, 1966.

Gruetzmacher, G., *Synesios von Kyrene.* Ein Charakterbild aus dem Untergang des Hellenentums. Leipzig, 1913.

Hagen, W., *Künstliche Traumerzeugung oder die Kunst, das Traumleben
nach eignem Wunsch zu lenken und zu beeinflussen.* Berlin, no date.

Hall, C. S., *The Meaning of Dreams.* New York, 1966.

Hall, C. S., and Van de Castle, R. L., *The Content Analysis of Dreams.*
New York, 1966.

Hall, C. C., and Lind, R. E., *Dreams, Life, and Literature.* Chapel Hill,
1970.

Hamilton, M., *Incubation or the Cure of Disease in Pagan Temples and Christian Churches*. London, 1906.
Hart, D., *Der tiefenpsychologische Begriff der Kompensation*. Dissertation, Zürich, 1956.
Hartmann, E., *The Biology of Dreaming*. Springfield, 1967.
Haupt, S. O., *Wirkt die Tragödie auf das Gemüt oder den Verstand oder die Moralität der Zuschauer? oder Der aus den Schriften des Aristoteles erbrachte wissenschaftliche Beweis für die intellektualistische Bedeutung von «Katharsis»*. Berlin, 1915.
Heimann, B., *Die Tiefschlafspekulation der alten Upanishaden*. Untersuchungen zur Geschichte des Buddhismus VII. Munich, 1922.
Hennings, J. C., *Von den Ahnungen und Visionen*. Leipzig, 1777.
Henry-Couannier, M., *Saint François de Sales et ses amitiés*. Paris and Brussels, 1956.
Hentze, C., *Das Haus als Weltort der Seele*. Stuttgart, 1961.
Heraklit, fragm. ed. B. Snell. Munich, 1926.
Herzog, R., *Die Wunderheilungen von Epidauros*, Philologus, Supplement-Volume XXII, booklet III. Leipzig, 1931.
Hill, B., ed., *Such Stuff as Dreams*. London, 1967.
Hoche, A., *Das träumende Ich*. Jena, 1927.
von Hofmannsthal, H., *Ariadne auf Naxos*. 1912.
Huxley, A., *The Devils of Loudun*. London, 1952.
——— *The Doors of Perception*. London, 1954.
Jackson, J. H., *Selected Writings*, ed. James Taylor, 2 volumes. London, 1958.
Jacob, G., *Märchen und Traum*. Hanover, 1923.
Janet, P., *L'état mental des hystériques*. Paris, 1893–94.
——— *Les oscillations du niveau mental*. Nouveau traité de psychologie. Volume IV, F.3. Paris, 1937.
Jessen, P., *Versuch einer wissenschaftlichen Begründung der Psychologie*. Berlin, 1855.
Jezower, I., *Das Buch der Träume*. Berlin, 1928.
Johnson, A., *Dream-Analysis*. Glasgow, 1918.
Jones, R. M., *Ego Synthesis in Dreams*. Cambridge, Mass., 1962.
——— *The New Psychology of Dreaming*. New York and London, 1970.
Jung, C. G., "On the Psychology and Pathology of So-Called Occult Phenomena." *CW* 1. Zurich dissertation. German original, Leipzig, 1902.
——— *Collected Papers on Analytical Psychology*. London, 1916.
——— *Psychological Types*. *CW* 6. German original, 1921.
——— "Association, Dream, and Hysterical Symptom." *CW* 2. German original, 1906.
——— "On the Significance of Number Dreams." *CW* 4. German original, 1910–11.
——— "General Aspects of Dream Psychology." *CW* 8. German original, 1916.

—— "The Practical Use of Dream-Analysis." *CW* 16. German original, 1934.

—— "A Review of the Complex Theory." *CW* 8. German original, 1934.

—— "Traumsymbole des Individuationsprozesses." Eranos Yearbook. *CW* 12.

—— "Psychology and Religion." *CW* 11. German original, 1940.

—— "Zur Methodik; einführende Thesen." Manuscript in possession of C. A. Meier.

—— *Psychology and Alchemy. CW* 12. German original, 1944.

—— "On the Nature of Dreams." *CW* 8. German original, 1945.

—— "Synchronicity: An Acausal Connecting Principle." *CW* 8. German original, 1952.

—— "On Psychic Energy." *CW* 8. German original, 1948.

—— *Memories, Dreams, Reflections.* New York, 1963.

Jung, C. G., and Pauli, W., *Naturerklärung und Psyche.* Studien aus dem C. G. Jung-Institut. Zürich, 1952.

Jung, C. G., and Wilhelm, R., *The Secret of the Golden Flower.* Munich, 1929.

Jung, J. H., *Theorie der Geister-Kunde in einer natur-, vernunft- und bibelmäßigen Beantwortung der Frage: was Ahnungen, Gesichten und Geistererscheinungen geglaubt und nicht geglaubt werden müßte.* Leipzig, 1903.

Kales, A., ed., *Sleep Physiology and Pathology.* Philadelphia and Toronto, 1969.

Kehrer, R. A., *Wach- und Wahrträumen bei Gesunden und Kranken.* Leipzig, 1945.

Kelchner, G. D., *Dreams in Old Norse Literature and Their Affinities in Folklore.* Cambridge, 1935.

Keller, G., *Das Tagebuch und das Traumbuch.* Basel, 1942.

Kelser, M. T., *Dreams the Dark Speech of the Spirit.* New York, 1970.

Kerenyi, K., *Mythologie der Griechen.* Zürich, 1951.

—— *The Heroes of the Greeks.* New York and London, 1978. German original, 1958.

Kety, S., Evarts, E. V., and Williams, W. L., eds., "Sleep and Altered States of Consciousness," *Proc. Ass. Res. in Nervous and Mental Disease*, Vol. 14. Baltimore, 1967.

Kiessig, M., ed., *Dichter erzählen ihre Träume.* Selbstzeugnisse deutscher Dichter aus zwei Jahrhunderten. Düsseldorf and Cologne, 1964.

Kleitman, N., *Sleep and Wakefulness.* Chicago and London, 1963.

König-Fachsenfeld, O., *Wandlungen des Traumproblems von der Romantik bis zur Gegenwart.* Stuttgart, 1935.

Kraepelin, E., *Die Sprachstörungen im Traum.* Leipzig, 1906.

Kramer, M., ed., *Dream Psychology and the New Biology of Dreaming.* Springfield, 1969.

Krüger, J. G., *Joh. Gottlob Krügers Träume*. Opus aureum de quidditate idditatis iussu Apollinis editum...sowie eine Übersetzung aus den cérémonies et coutumes religieuses de tous les peuples du monde. Halle im Magdeburgischen, 1765.

Künigsperger, J., *Kalender von allerhandt artzney*. Augsburg, 1539.

Lacombrade, C., *Synesios de Cyrène*. Paris, 1951.

Ladd, G. T., "Contribution to the Psychology of Visual Dreams," *Mind*. London, 1892.

Lang, A., *The Book of Dreams and Ghosts*. London, 1897.

Lang, W., *Das Traumbuch des Synesius von Kyrene*. Tübingen, 1926.

Lauer, Ch., "Das Wesen des Traumes in der Beurteilung der talmudischen und rabbinischen Literatur," *Internationale Zeitschrift für Ärztliche Psychoanalyse*.

Lazari, D., *Dyonysii Lazari...tractatulus de somniis*. Venice, 1606.

Leander, R., *Träumereien an französischen Kaminen*. Leipzig, 1871.

Leisegang, H., *Pneuma hagion; der Ursprung des Geistbegriffs der synopt. Evangelien aus der griechischen Mystik*. Leipzig, 1922.

Leonhard, K., *Die Gesetze des normalen Träumens*. Leipzig, 1939.

Lersch, Ph., *Der Traum in der deutschen Romantik*. Munich, 1923.

Lewis, N.D.C., and Landis, C., "Freud's Library," in *The Psychoanalytic Review*.

Linke, H., *Über Macrobius' Kommentar zu Ciceros Somnium Scipionis*, Philologische Abhandlungen, Berlin.

Loomis, A. L., Harvey, E. N. and Hobart, G. A., "Cerebral States During Sleep as Studied by Human Brain Potentials," *Journal Experimental Psychology*.

Luce, G. G., *Current Research on Sleep and Dreams*. U.S. Department of Health, Education, and Welfare, without date.

Ludwig, A., *Die Schrift «peri enhypnion» des Synesius von Kyrene*, Psychische Studien, Leipzig.

Lungwitz, H., *Das Träumen als geistig-seelische Nachtarbeit*. Halle, 1938.

MacKenzie, N., *Dreams and Dreaming*. London, 1965.

Macleod, F., *Das Reich der Träume*. Jena and Leipzig, 1905.

Macnish, R., *Der Schlaf in allen seinen Gestalten*. Leipzig, 1835.

Macrobius, *Commentary on the Dream of Scipio*. New York, 1952.

―――― *Macrobii Aurelii Theodosii in somnium Scipionis libri* II; *saturnaliorum libri* VII; *nunc denuo recogniti et multis in locis aucti*. Lugduni, 1538.

―――― *Aur. Theodosii Macrobii opera ad optimas editiones collata; praemittitur notitia literaria; ed accurata*. Biponti, 1788.

―――― *Les saturnales*. Paris, no date.

Maeterlinck, M., *Deux contes: Le massacre des innocents—Onirologie*. Paris, 1918.

Mahoney, M. F., *The Meaning in Dreams and Dreaming. The Jungian Viewpoint*. New York, 1966.

Marmor, J., "Psychoanalytic Therapy as an Educational Process," Masserman, J., ed., *Science and Psychoanalysis*, vol. 5. New York, 1962.
——— "Psychoanalytic Therapy and Theories of Learning," Masserman, J., ed., *Science and Psychoanalysis*, Vol. 7. New York, 1964.
——— "Limitations of Free Association," *Arch. Gen. Psychiat.* vol. 22, 1970.
Marrou, H. I., "Synesios of Cyrene and Alexandrian Neoplatonism," *The Conflict Between Paganism and Christianity in the Fourth Century*, ed. Momigliano (Oxford-Warburg Studies). Oxford, 1963.
Maury, A., *Le sommeil et les rêves*. Paris, 1865.
Mayer, F., *Die Struktur des Traumes*. Haag, 1937.
Meier, C. A., *Ancient Incubation and Modern Psychotherapy*. Evanston, 1967. German original, 1949.
——— *The Unconscious in Its Empirical Manifestations*, Boston, 1984. German original, 1968.
——— *A Jungian View. Dream Psychology and the New Biology of Dreaming*, ed. M. Kramer. Springfield, Ill., 1969.
——— *Zeitgemässe Probleme der Traumforschung*, Kultur- und staatswiss. Schr. ETH, Zürich.
——— "Psychosomatik in Jungscher Sicht," *Psyche*, Stuttgart.
——— "Spontanmanifestationen des kollektiven Unbewussten," *Zbl. f. Psychother.*, Leipzig.
——— "Psychosomatic Medicine from the Jungian Point of View," *Journal Analytic Psychology*, London.
Meier, C. A., Ruef, H., Ziegler, A. and Hall, C. C., "Forgetting of Dreams in the Laboratory," *Perceptual and Motor Skills*.
Meier, G. F., *Versuch der Erklärung des Nachtwandelns*. Halle, 1758.
Michelsen, K., *Neun Träume*. Leipzig, 1892.
'Migne, Patrol. Graec. Lat. tom. 66.
Müller, J., *Über die phantastischen Gesichtserscheinungen* (reprint). Munich, 1967.
von Negelein, J., *Der Traumschlüssel des Jagaddeva*. Giessen, 1912.
Nerol, T., *Sepher Haolamoth sive Opus encyklopadeicum tripertitium Hebraice*. Venice, 1707–08.
Nietzsche, F., *Die Geburt der Tragödie*. 1870–71.
——— *Menschliches, Allzumenschliches*. 1876–78.
——— *Morgenröte*. 1880–81.
Normann, R., *Die Symbolik des Traumes*. Prien, 1923.
Oppenheim, A. L., "The Interpretation of Dreams in the Ancient Near East," *Transact. Amer. Philos. Soc.*, Philadelphia.
Oswald, I., *Sleeping and Waking*. Amsterdam and New York, 1962.
Pack, R. A., *Artemidori Daldiani, Onirocriticon Libri* v, *Bibliotheca Teubneriana*. Leipzig, 1963.
Pauli, W., "Die philosophische Bedeutung der Idee der Komplementarität," *Experientia*, Basel.

Pererius, B., *De magia, de observatione somniorum, et de divinatione astrologica libri tres; adversus fallaces et superstitiosas artes.* Coloniae Agrippinae, apud Ioannem Gymnicum, 1598.

Peucer, C., *Commentarius de praecipuis divinationum generibus, in quo a prophetis divina autoritate traditis, et physicis praedictionibus, separantur diabolicae fraudes et superstitiosae observationes.* Wittenberg, 1553.

Prince, M., *The Dissociation of a Personality.* London, 1905.

Purkinje, J. E., *Wachen, Schlaf und verwandte Zustände.* Handwörterbuch der Physiologie mit Rüchsicht auf physiologische Pathologie, ed. Rudolf Wagner, Volum III., Braunschweig, 1846.

Radestock, P., *Schlaf und Traum.* Leipzig, 1879.

Ramanuja, *Siddhanta.* Ein Kommentar zu den Brahmasutras. Jena, 1917.

Ratcliff, A.J.J., *A History of Dreams: A Brief Account of the Evolution of Dream Theories, with a Chapter on the Dream in Literature.* Boston, 1923.

———— *Traum und Schicksal.* Dresden, 1925.

Reinacher, E., *An den Schlaf.* Stuttgart, 1939.

Reinhardt, K., *Platons Mythen.* Bonn, 1927.

Reitzenstein, R., *Die hellenistischen Mysterienreligionen.* Leipzig, 1927.

Rivers, W.H.R., *Conflict and Dream.* London, 1923.

Roscher, W. H., *Ausführliches Lexikon der griechischen und römischen Mythologie.* Leipzig, 1884–1893.

Rosenkranz, J.K.F., *Psychologie oder die Wissenschaft vom subjektiven Geist.* 2. Aufl. Königsberg, 1843.

Rousselle, E., *Seelische Führung im lebenden Taoismus*, Eranos Yearbook, Zürich, 1954.

Sanctis, S., *I Sogni.* Studi psicologici e clinici di un alienista. Turin, 1899.

———— *Nuovi contributi alla psicofisiologia del sogno.* Bologna, 1933.

———— *Psychologie des Traumes.* Munich.

Sauneron, S., *Les Songes et leur interprétation; Egypte ancienne, Babylone, Hittites, Canaan, Israel, Islam, Peuples altaiques, Persans, Kurdes, Inde, Cambodge, Chine, Japon.* Paris, 1959.

Scarlatini, O., *L'huomo, e sue parti figurato, e simbolico, Anatomico, Rationale, Morale, Mistico, Politico, e Legale*, etc., with many prints. Bologna, 1684.

Schär, H., *«Bemerkungen zu Träumen der Bibel», Traum und Symbol.* Neuere Arbeiten zur analytischen Psychologie C. G. Jungs. Zürich, 1963.

Schedler, M., *Die Philosophie des Macrobius und ihr Einfluß auf die Wissenschaft des christlichen Mittelalters.* Beiträge zur Geschichte der Philosophie des Mittelalters, Texte und Untersuchungen. Munich, 1916.

von Schelling, F.W.J., *Werke* ɪ. Augsburg, 1858.

Scherner, K. A., *Das Leben des Traumes.* Berlin, 1861.

Schleich, K. L., *Wir schlafen zu wenig.* Basel.

Schopenhauer, A., *Versuch über Geistersehen und was damit zusammen-hängt* (Parerga und Paralipomena).
Schrötter, K., "Experimentelle Träume," *Zbl. Psychoanal.*, Wiesbaden.
Schubert, G. H., *Die Symbolik des Traumes*. Leipzig, 1840.
Seafield, F., *The Literature and Curiosities of Dreams. A Commonplace Book of Speculations Concerning the Mystery of Dreams and Visions, Records of Curious and Well-Authenticated Dreams, and Notes on the Various Modes of Interpretation Adopted in Ancient and Modern times*. London, 1865.
Servadio, E., "Ein paranormaler Traum in der analytischen Situation," *Zs. Parapsychol. Grenzgeb. Psychol.*, Bern.
Shurley, J. T., "Profound Experimental Sensory Isolation," *American Journal Psychiatry*.
von Siebenthal, W., *Die Wissenschaft vom Traum*. Berlin, 1953.
Silberer, H., "Zur Charakteristik des lekanomantischen Schauens," *Zbl. Psychoanal.*, Wiesbaden.
——— "Lekanomantische Versuche," *Zbl. Psychoanal.*, Wiesbaden.
——— "Zur Frage der Spermatozoenträume," *Jb. Psychoanal. Psychopathol. Forschungen*, Leipzig and Vienna.
——— *Probleme der Mystik und ihrer Symbolik*. Leipzig, 1914.
——— "Symbolik des Erwachens und Schwellensymbolik überhaupt," *Jb. Psychoanal. Psychopathol. Forschungen*, Leipzig and Vienna.
——— *Der Traum*. Stuttgart, 1919.
Silberstein, A., *Die Katharsis des Aristoteles*. Leipzig, 1867.
Simon, P. M., *Le monde des rêves*; le rêve, l'hallucination, le somnambulisme et l'hypnotisme, l'illusion, les paradis artificiels, le ragle, le cerveau et le rêve. Paris, 1888.
Sogni e Cabala del Lotto. No Author, Supplemento No. 45 a Cronaca. Rom, 1970.
Sonnet, A., *Die rätselhafte Welt der Träume*. Heidenheim, 1959.
Spitta, H., *Die Schlaf- und Traumzustände der menschlichen Seele*. Freiburg i.B. 1892, 2nd edition.
Splittgerber, F., *Schlaf und Tod*. Halle, 1865.
Stahl, W. H., ed., Macrobius, *Commentary on the Dream of Scipio*. New York, 1952.
Stahr, A., *Aristoteles und die Wirkung der Tragödie*. Berlin, 1859.
Stevenson, R. L., *Across the Plains with other Memories and Essays*. London, 1905.
Struempell, L., *Die Natur und Entstehung der Träume*. Leipzig, 1874.
Los Suenos y las Sociedades humanas. Buenos Aires, 1964.
Synesius von Kyrene, *Traktat Peri enhypnion*. Venice 1516 and 1518, Lyon, 1549, Paris 1586 and 1612.
Babylonischer Talmud. Tr. Berachoth 55a.
Tart, Ch. T., ed., *Altered States of Consciousness*. New York and London, 1969.
Tertullianus, *De anima*. ed. J. H. Waszink. Amsterdam, 1947.

Thorndike, L., *A History of Magic and Experimental Science*. VIII. vols. New York, 1929–1958.

Tissie, P., *Les rêves; physiologie et pathologie*. Paris, 1898.

Traugott, R., *Der Traum psychologisch und kulturgeschichtlich betrachtet*. Würzburg, 1913.

Traumbuch Arach. Salzburg, 1959.

Troxler, I.P.V., *Blick in das Wesen des Menschen*. 1812.

Uslar, D., *Der Traum als Welt; Untersuchungen zur Ontologie und Phänomenologie des Traumes*. Pfullingen, 1964.

Vaschide, N., *Le sommeil et les rêves*. Paris, 1911.

Veronese, F., *Saggio di una fisiologia del sonno, del sogno e dei processi affini*. Reggio-Emiliana 1910.

Vetter, A., *Die Zeichensprache von Schrift und Traum*. Freiburg and Munich, 1970.

Vischer, F. Th., *Auch Einer*. 2 Volumes, 1879.

Vold, J. M., *Über den Traum*. Leipzig 1910 and 1912.

Volkmann, R., *Synesius von Kyrene*. Berlin, 1869.

Webb, W. B., *Sleep: An experimental Approach*. New York and London, 1968.

Weill, A., *Qu'est-ce que le rêve?* Paris, 1872.

Weiss, H. B., *Oneirocritica americana*. New York, 1944.

Wilhelm, R., and Jung, C. G., *The Secret of the Golden Flower*. Munich, 1929.

Wolf, F. A., Vermischte Schriften und Aufsätze in lateinischer und deutscher Sprache. Halle, 1802.

Wolff, W., *The Dream-Mirror of Conscience. A History of Dream Interpretation from 2000 B.C. and a New Theory of Dream Synthesis*. New York, 1952.

Woodroffe, J., *The Garland of Letters*. Madras, 1955.

Zimmer, H., *Abenteuer und Fahrten der Seele*. Zürich, 1961.

INDEX

Other Titles from Sigo Press

The Unholy Bible *by June Singer*

Emotional Child Abuse *by Joel Covitz*

Dreams of a Woman *by Shelia Moon*

Androgyny *by June Singer*

The Dream-The Vision of the Night *by Max Zeller*

Sandplay Studies *by Bradway et al.*

Symbols Come Alive in the Sand *by Evelyn Dundas*

Inner World of Childhood *by Frances G. Wickes*

Inner World of Man *by Frances G. Wickes*

Inner World of Choice *by Frances G. Wickes*

Available from SIGO PRESS, 25 New Chardon Street, #8748A, Boston, Massachusetts, 02114. tel. (617) 526-7064

In England: Element Books, Ltd., Longmead, Shaftesbury, Dorset, SP7 8PL. tel. (0747) 51339, Shaftesbury.